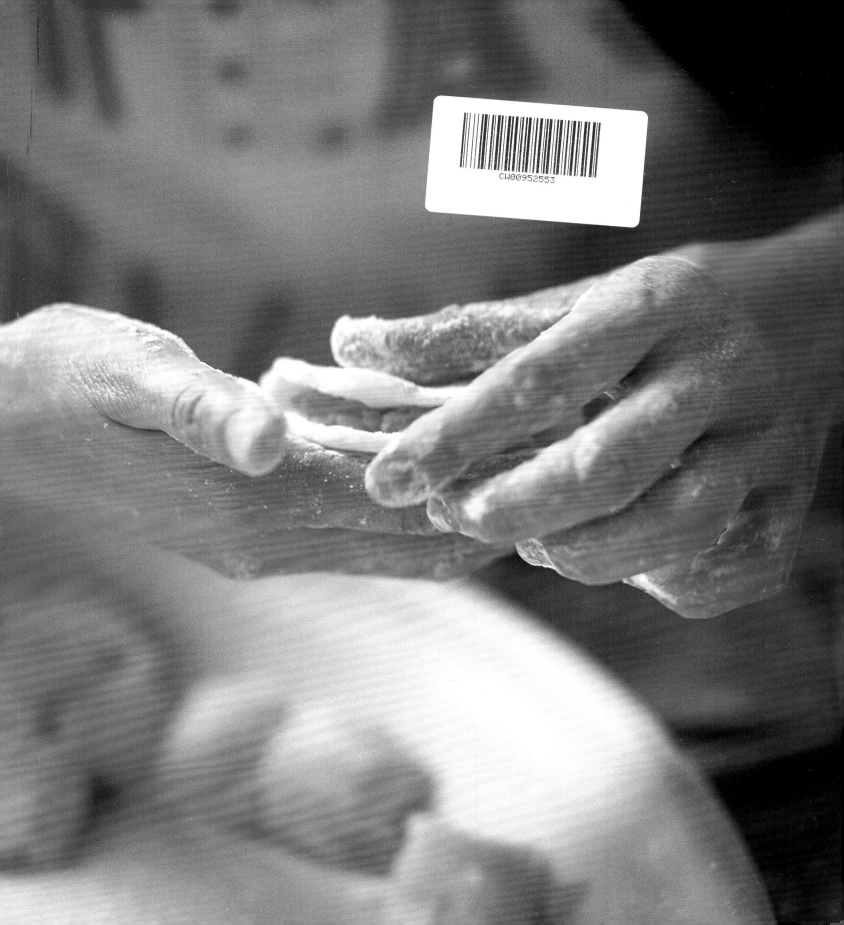

Shiok!

Exciting Tropical Asian Flavors

by Terry Tan and Christopher Tan
foreword by David Thompson
photography by Edmond Ho

PERIPLUS

I had the good fortune of growing up in an extended family, with any numbers of surrogate mothers, unexplained aunts and uncles and cousins, and neighbors who enriched my life with a multitude of culinary gems. To them I dedicate this book; may it be embraced by future generations of Singaporeans with the same passion. – *Terry Tan*

This book is for my grandmother, whose *kueh bangket* are without equal, and my mother, whose *kueh lapis* is without peer. To God be the glory. – *Christopher Tan*

Published by Periplus Editions, with editorial offices at
130 Joo Seng Road #06-01, Singapore 368357

Copyright © 2003 Periplus Editions (HK) Ltd.
All rights reserved.
ISBN: 0-7946-0223-1 (hardcover)
        0-7946-0095-6 (paperback)

Distributors:
North America, Latin America, and Europe
Tuttle Publishing, 364 Innovation Drive,
North Clarendon, VT 05759-9436, USA
Tel (802) 773 8930; fax (802) 773 6993
email: info@tuttlepublishing.com
www.tuttlepublishing.com

Japan, Tuttle Publishing
Yaekari Building, 3F, 5-4-12
Osaki, Shinagawa-Ku, Tokyo 141 0032, Japan
Tel (813) 5437 0171; fax (813) 5437 0755
email: tuttle-sales@gol.com

Asia Pacific, Berkeley Books Pte Ltd
130 Joo Seng Road #06-01, Singapore 368357
Tel (65) 6280 1330; fax (65) 6280 6290
email: inquiries@periplus.com.sg

Contents

a deep-seated passion for food

Call me biased, but I think the best reason for visiting Singapore is the food. If Singaporeans aren't eating a meal, then they are either talking about it or planning for the next. This passion does not stem merely from some culinary hedonism — although pleasure surely plays a large part — but from some deep-seated belief that the sharing of food and its preparation binds a family and community together. Even more so when the food tastes so good.

Perhaps the true strength of Singaporean food lies in its diverse background and the willingness of the people to embrace new tastes and ingredients. Chinese, Malay, Indian, and Nonya cuisines are both maintained and blended into one of the world's most interesting, delicious cuisines. Whatever the reason the result is food that tastes … *shiok*!

The Jackfruit Curry and Gulai Prawns make me want to go to the market and then into the kitchen. The Fishhead Curry could easily do a winning lap on Race Course Road. The Satay or Hainanese Chicken Rice are happily reminiscent of that served in the old Beach Road or Middle Road restaurants. In this book, culinary favorites such as these are presented in an enticing style with truly alluring photographs.

I have known both Terry and Christopher Tan for several years and have always been impressed with their conviction and knowledge. This wonderful book is the outcome.

David Thompson

shiok! (she'iok) (adj.)
sublime, unutterably wonderful, greatly more than satisfactory in all ways, unsurpassably good

Some wag once said that the quickest way to start a debate in Singapore is to walk up to a random group of people and ask them, "So where can I get the best chicken rice?"

Eating is the Singapore national sport. An irresistible vein of foodieness runs deep in the Singaporean genetic makeup. We plan lunch over breakfast and dinner over lunch, and then go out to supper. We incessantly trade tips about the best places to get the *shiokest* dishes. Our Chinese wedding dinners stretch to nine courses over four hours. We endure forty minutes of queueing for a simple bowl of minced pork noodles with black vinegar. Why? Because we can't find the particular savor of the stall's old-fashioned chili sauce anywhere else.

There is a such diversity of ways and places to stuff your face here, from hawker centers and corner coffeeshops to the classiest contemporary Asian and Western restaurants. You can empty your wallet for a French dinner one night and sit down to a $1 *dosai* (south Indian rice crêpe) the next morning. Given the details of our island republic's history, our egalitarian omnivorousness is no surprise. Over the centuries before and since its founding in 1819 by the Englishman Sir Stamford Raffles, Singapore has had a cultural life braided with Chinese, Malay, Arab, Thai, Indian, Indonesian, Eurasian, colonial British, and continental influences. Our cuisine, then and now, reflects this. How else to explain a Chinese chicken soup with macaroni, crispy shallots, and fried bread croutons? A rich curry of pork ribs and bamboo shoots? A Hainanese chef's special "chicken cutlets" in HP Sauce-spiked brown gravy with chips and peas? A staple breakfast trio of hot buttered toast slathered with coconut-egg jam, a soft-boiled egg drizzled with dark soy sauce, and a cup of thick, black, highly sweetened coffee? When you grow up with such an eclectic mix of edibles, your taste buds get a uniquely intoxicating education.

Chinese Cooking: Dialectic Differences Forget the greasy homogeneity of the oriental take-away menu too often found abroad. The true diversity of Chinese cuisine is as wide and deep as regional French or Italian. There is no "Chinese food" *per se* — there is food from Hunan and Swatow and Beijing and Yunnan and Shanghai and that's without considering the web of Chinese ancestry extending throughout Southeast Asia, the Thai-Teochews, Indonesian Chinese, and so on, each strand of which has its own culinary distinctions.

Terry comes from the match of an Indonesian Chinese father and a mother whose antecedents came from the early Peranakan clans of Malacca, Penang, and Thailand. Then again, his father's family also had Hokkien roots in China's Fujian Province, and his mother's family a branch of good Teochew stock from Swatow Province. Every family feast was a glorious *tok panjang* — the Peranakan festive offering of dishes spread across a long table. Chris's maternal grandfather was a true-blue baba who married a true-blue Cantonese lady, and their household meals were an eclectic mix of classics from both worlds, brought together in a mouth-watering alchemy.

In essence, Chinese food in Singapore has four main regional branches — Hokkien, Teochew Cantonese, and Hainanese. Teochews are inordinately fond of soups, braised dishes, and

opposite: Beautifully mottled flower-crab shells.
previous page: Chinese chives tipped with jade-green buds.
page 1: Dumplings being shaped from glutinous rice dough.

steamed dishes, clear, and relatively unadorned. Hokkiens stir up delicious noodle dishes and meat rolls. And the Cantonese are past masters at roasted meats and simply sauced vegetables and seafood. The most celebrated contribution of the Hainanese, apart from the scores of *ah kors* or male chefs who manned the woks and ovens of country club kitchens and Western restaurants — some of whom still do today — is the aforementioned chicken rice, which by now has evolved into something quite different from the original dish cooked on Hainan Island.

These précis do not of course do full justice to the true range of regional Chinese cuisines, which is displayed as much in home kitchens as in restaurants. Other Chinese styles of cooking, such as Shanghai, Hunan, Sichuan, and such only noticeably established themselves as part of the local landscape from the mid-1950s onwards, as Chinese from those parts migrated here. Much in evidence these days are contemporary strains of Chinese cooking informed by Hong Kong-style Cantonese cuisine, French techniques, and the occasional Southeast Asian flavor, which have a great sense of adventure and vibrancy to them.

Malay Flavors: Rasa Sayang Malay cooking has a revered — though not always loudly acknowledged — place within the Singapore kitchen as a major evolutionary influence, in the same way Indian and Indonesian cuisines do. The fresh spices and herbs of the Malaysian peninsula and the dry, aromatic ones of Arabic Muslim and Indian Muslim influences combine in the intricate weave of local Malay food. Who has eaten *nasi lemak* and not remembered its delicate nuances? Some of Terry's fondest childhood memories are of our neighbourhood Malay hawkers who sold little banana leaf packets of this coconut rice, topped with *sambal ikan bilis* (baby anchovies), a fried egg and a rich, hot *sambal goreng* to dab on it all. And there are still few satays to beat those made by Malay chefs, Terry's favorite being *satay babat*, made with tripe. The rich continuity of coconut, palm sugar, and rice flour between Indonesian and peninsular Malay desserts has also left its mark on Nonya sweets.

Indian Influences: Spice-laden Breezes Historically, most of Singapore's Indian inhabitants came from the south of the sub-continent — Tamils and Malayalees mainly. Later came the Sindis, Gujaratis, Bengalis, and Punjabis from the northern provinces, and presently the square kilometer that makes up Little India is redolent with their combined gastronomical talents. It is

Below, left to right: Deep-fried "butterfly" buns; used condensed milk cans make handy takeaway coffee cups; fish seller at the Chinatown Complex market; *otak-otak*, or barbecued fish in banana leaves.

a disservice to summarize India's cuisines in anything less than several hundred pages, but as a rough reference for the palate, southern Indian food in Singapore is characterized by rice flour based breads as well as rice dishes, with an abundance of seafood, fresh vegetables, cool yoghurt, and sour tamarind as foils for aromatic, chili-hot spice blends spiked with mustard seeds and curry leaves. Northern Indian food here calls more often on wheat breads as staples, and boasts many rich and complex curries as well as tandoori specialties. A meal of either ilk is typically built around a mix of dry and wet dishes, and chutneys and pickles. One "Indian" curry, made with large fish heads in a spicy, sour gravy, is in fact a uniquely Singaporean variation on a Keralan theme that you won't find in the motherland.

Peranakan roots: Our Own Fusion Heritage Also known as Straits Chinese, the latter meaning "born of the soil," the Peranakan people have roots in Chinese, Malay, and Indian culture — the respectful term for Peranakan men, *baba*, comes from an Indian word; women are called *nonyas*. The original community arose centuries ago in Malacca, and today the other centers of the diaspora are in Penang and Singapore, with small groups in Indonesia and Thailand. Each community has its own distinct culinary emphases. Malaccan and Singaporean Nonya food is largely similar, but many Nonya dishes from Penang, further north, have a Thai mood about them, and Penangite patois embraces many Thai words. Many Peranakans were of Chinese-Indonesian parentage, like my father; the nearby Riau Islands were a Peranakan outpost.

All told, it makes for scrumptious eating. A natural example of "fusion" cuisine — without any of the hapless connotations that word has gathered in the modern era, if you please. The Peranakan culinary canon integrates its diverse roots into a glorious whole. It includes curries of seafood, beef, and chicken, but also pork; braised meats almost purely Chinese in style, but enlivened with a snap of spices; fattening festive noodle dishes and healthy salads of raw vegetables and herbs; and rich desserts that will have you napping after lunch. Perhaps its most iconic dish is chicken and pork ribs cooked in a spicy tamarind gravy with *buah keluak*, Indonesian black nuts whose meat tastes divinely like the offspring of a black truffle, a dark chocolate bar and wet earth after rain.

The best Nonya cooks, like cooks everywhere, measure ingredients and cooking times with their hands, eyes, noses, and ears, and they give a name to this cooking by feel: *agak-agak*.

Below, left to right: Vegetables bagged for sale; man serving up chicken curry at the Adam Road food center; a well-connected roast meat stall at the Tiong Barhu food center; durian, the king of fruits.

Much of Terry's own style in this respect was handed down to him by first his grandmother and then his mother, bless their Nonya souls, who in assigning him sometimes tedious kitchen tasks made him an unwitting trustee of the culture. Chris was not forcibly steeped in his ancestry in the same way, but picked it up mostly through osmosis, as it were.

As food writers, our sense of our heritage reminds us that we have a duty to arouse curiosity and passion about food culture in future generations, to instill a respect for tradition as well as a level-headed appreciation for innovation. We must all learn to care about our food traditions enough to prevent them slipping away, to keep the precious legacy of our parents' and grand-parents' kitchens alive and bright. We hope that this book will spur you on to do that.

How To Use This Book

This book was written for three kinds of people. One is the Singaporean who doesn't cook much, but wants to get to know his own food heritage better. The second is the intrepid non-Singaporean who wants to broaden his culinary horizons. Welcome to our world! The third is everyone else. Why would one want to miss out on great food?

If your desire to stir up something delicious is tempered by a vague idea of cooking as a complex, tedious process and therefore a dreaded chore, be reassured that none of these recipes are particu-larly difficult. A few require a dedicated investment of time, and all benefit from your full attention — the unexamined dish is not worth eating, after all — but, trust us, the returns are worth it.

Cooking once was more laborious, true. Buying a chicken also used to mean killing, de-feathering, blood-letting, and butchering it. Terry has severed his fair share of chickens' jugulars, scoured neighborhood hedges for the *bunga telang* flowers his mother would press a dark blue-purple dye from to color her *ang koo kueh* (mung bean and rice flour cakes), and taken countless bus rides to the seashore to gather, at low tide, tons of wet, slimy, icky seaweed to be dried in the sun, boiled down, clarified, and cooked with sugar and water to make delicious agar-agar jelly for Chinese New Year.

But that was long ago. Nowadays, you don't have to coax damp wood to make a fire in a *hung lo* (earthenware) oven — a museum piece nowadays — or grind your own rice flour, or even peel your own shallots (though it does build character). Shopping for and cooking local food can be a source of pure pleasure. We urge you to take the time to explore your local wet market. Smell the herbs, pat the vegetables, watch the butchers and fishmongers carve up their charges, and above all chit-chat with the stallholders and their regular customers, who are invariably founts of culinary information. You will learn, if you haven't already, how to choose fruit and vegetables, how to appraise seafood with a wise eye, what this spice and that gourd is for, how to best portion a chicken for a family of five. This is knowledge not on sale at the supermarket, which though convenient and clean — and fast, if you're pressed for time — lacks the sheer exuberance of the open-air Asian *pasar*.

Chris, an former psychology student, likes to think of cooking as therapy; the sequence of shopping, assembling, prepping, and following the final sequence of steps is a contemplative, creative and deeply satisfying activity. Taking a recipe and experimenting with it until it has gotten under your skin requires no less art and gives no less joy than learning to play a Chopin etude. We urge you to *agak-agak*, to judge, and adjust quantities of ingredients on the fly, to imbue the dishes with your own personal touch.

This collection of recipes is a personal and idiosyncratic one. It is not meant to be a definitive guide to Singaporean gastronomy — as if such a thing could be contained in a single volume! — nor is it an anonymous collation of ersatz ethnic expressions packaged for painless digestion. These dishes are drawn from our lives, from the home repertoires we have cooked our way through many times over the years. They are what we enjoy eating. We hope you find them *shiok* too!

Opposite: Intense heat produces intense flavor.

Sambals, Achars, Chutneys and Sauces

Among all the things Singaporeans are notorious for, one is absolutely true. You can always spot a group of Singaporean tourists on holiday in the Northern hemisphere, not by the "lahs" that pepper the conversation, not by the ruthless efficiency with which they bargain for souvenirs — but by their jars of home-made *sambal*, smuggled past Customs in a plastic bag tied with a rubber band, which they pass around surreptitiously when confronted with a bland buffet of foreign food.

    This chapter, which could potentially be infinitely long, is devoted to the accompaniments and condiments that make the Singaporean meal the endlessly stimulating mix that it is.

Hoi Sin, Wine, and Sesame Oil Marinade

1 tablespoon hoi sin sauce
4 tablespoons Shaoxing rice wine
1 tablespoon sesame oil
1 tablespoon finely crushed garlic
1 teaspoon black pepper
1 tablespoon dark soy sauce

1 Blend all ingredients well. Use as a marinade for whole joints of pork, pork fillet, or chicken, before roasting.

Makes 115 ml (scant 1/2 cup) marinade
Preparation time: 5 minutes

Hoi Sin, Oyster and Worcestershire Sauce Marinade

2 tablespoons hoi sin sauce
2 tablespoons oyster sauce
1 tablespoon Worcestershire sauce
2 tablespoons water

1 Blend all ingredients well. Use as a marinade for barbecued spare ribs or fried chicken.

Makes 100 ml (scant 1/2 cup) marinade
Preparation time: 5 minutes

Wine, Oyster Sauce, and Sesame Oil Marinade

4 tablespoons Shaoxing rice wine
2 tablespoons oyster sauce
2 tablespoons sesame oil
1 tablespoon finely grated ginger
3 tablespoons water

1 Blend all ingredients. Use as a marinade for steamed chicken, as a base for braising pork or even as a sauce for stir-fried pork, beef, or liver.

Makes 180 ml (scant 3/4 cup) marinade
Preparation time: 5 minutes

Tamarind and Soy Sauce Marinade

A similar blend of flavors to the Filipino *adobo*.

2 tablespoons tamarind pulp
6 tablespoons water
2 tablespoons dark soy sauce
1 tablespoon sugar
2 teaspoon pepper
1 teaspoon salt

1 Knead tamarind with water until pulp is dissolved. Strain and mix with all other ingredients, stirring to dissolve sugar. Cool before using to marinate chicken pieces, sliced pork, or beef before braising or sautéing.

Makes 160 ml (2/3 cup) marinade
Preparation time: 5 minutes

Basic Garam Masala

Garam masala is a warm spice mix that should be fragrant and compelling — which is why the coriander and cumin are roasted whole before grinding, for the most heightened aroma.

3 tablespoons coriander seeds
2 tablespoons cumin seeds
2 teaspoons black peppercorns
1 teaspoon ground cardamom
1 teaspoon ground cinnamon
1 teaspoon ground clove
1 teaspoon ground nutmeg

1 Set a wok (preferably non-stick, or very well seasoned) over low heat. When wok is hot, dry-fry coriander seeds for 4 to 6 minutes, stirring continuously, until they are fragrant and have darkened very slightly. Scrape into a bowl.
2 Dry-fry cumin seeds for 2 to 3 minutes until fragrant. When both spices have cooled, grind in spice grinder with black pepper until fine. Add all remaining spices and whizz just to mix. Store in an air-tight jar in a dark, dry place.

Makes scant $1/2$ cup
Preparation time: 5 minutes

Meat Curry Powder

The Meat and Seafood Curry Powders are a time-saver if you have access to good quality ground spices (that is, those with use-by dates a long way off). That said, if you have the time — and a good spice grinder — it is worth purchasing each spice whole and dry-roasting them individually until they smell fragrant. When they have cooled, grind them together, then store airtight. Blend wet aromatics like ginger, garlic, and onions with curry powder to a smooth paste, to be fried in oil before adding your meat and liquid.

250 g (9 oz) ground coriander
100 g ($3^1/_2$ oz) ground cumin
50 g ($1^3/_4$ oz) ground fennel
30 g (1 oz) ground black pepper
30 g (1 oz) chili powder
30 g (1 oz) ground turmeric

1 teaspoon ground cinnamon
1 teaspoon ground cardamom
1 teaspoon ground cloves

1 Mix all ingredients together. Set a wok (preferably non-stick, or very well seasoned) over low heat. When wok is hot, add mixture and dry-fry, stirring continuously and thoroughly, for about 10 to 15 minutes, until spices start to release their aromatic oils. Do not let them scorch. When done, scrape into a bowl, and when cool, store in airtight jars in a dark, dry place.

Makes about 500 g (1 lb 2 oz)
Cooking time: 10–15 minutes

Seafood Curry Powder

1 Use the ingredients as for Meat Curry Powder, but omit cinnamon and reduce coriander to 200 g (7 oz), using the same method as above. Makes about 450 g (1 lb).
2 After dry-frying, add 1 teaspoon ground fenugreek and $1/_2$ teaspoon ground star anise.

Note There is some evidence that "curry powder" of the supermarket variety is in fact a British invention, and in truth, in and outside India, there is no single all-purpose blend used as a major component in different curries, though simpler mixtures like *garam masala* and *panch phoran* (Bengali five-spice mix) have multiple applications.

Curry powder should keep for up for three months. If you live in a humid climate, always check for any mold before using — moldy powder will have a musty, fetid, unpleasant smell.

Chili, Preserved Yellow Beans, and Lime Juice Dip

A salty and savory dip for steamed and boiled seafood.

3 tablespoons preserved yellow soybeans (*tau cheo*)
2 fresh red chilies, finely sliced
5 shallots, finely sliced
1 1/2 tablespoons freshly squeezed lime juice, or
  1 tablespoon distilled white vinegar
1 teaspoon sugar

1 Spoon soybeans into a small bowl. Drain off and discard most of the salty preserving liquid. Roughly mash beans and stir in chilies and shallots, followed by lime juice and sugar.

Serves 2–4
Preparation time: 5 mins

Red Coconut Chutney

A fiery chutney for South Indian breads and rice dishes.

5 dried red chilies
100 g (3 1/2 oz) freshly grated coconut
3 shallots, chopped
1 tablespoon chopped ginger
1/2 teaspoon salt
1/4 teaspoon sugar
2 tablespoons oil
1 teaspoon black mustard seeds
3 sprigs curry leaves, stalk discarded

1 Deseed 4 chilies and soak in warm water 10 minutes. Drain and combine with 2 tablespoons of the soaking water, coconut, shallots, ginger, salt, and sugar in a blender. Blend to a thick paste, then scrape into a heatproof bowl.
2 Heat oil in a small pan over medium-high heat. When hot, add mustard seeds, curry leaves and remaining red chili. Fry for 20 seconds, then pour over coconut mixture and stir to mix well. Serve immediately. Finish it within a day as it won't keep.

Serves 3–4
Cooking time: 30 seconds
Preparation time: 10 mins

Chili, Lime Juice, Fish Sauce, and Peanut Brittle Dip

Terry's original blend of Thai, Vietnamese, and Cantonese influences, ideal for spring rolls and fried foods.

4 red chillies
2 tablespoons freshly squeezed lime juice
1 tablespoon fish sauce
3 tablespoons crushed peanut brittle
1 teaspoon sugar

1 Chop chilies fine. Mix with all remaining ingredients.

Serves 2–3
Preparation time: 5 mins

Dried Shrimp, Chilies, Lime Juice, and Mint Dip

Ground dried shrimps — the best you can buy, please — are very compatible with chili-based dips. This makes a good base for a cucumber or pineapple side salad or *kerabu*; just mix a few spoonfuls with the chopped fruit.

3 tablespoons dried shrimps
4 red chilies
4 tablespoons freshly squeezed lime juice
2 teaspoons sugar
1 teaspoon fish sauce
1 teaspoon finely chopped mint
2 tablespoons water

1 Soak dried shrimps in hot water for 30 minutes, until soft. Drain thoroughly.
2 Grind shrimps fine with a pestle and mortar or mini-chopper. Add chilies and grind until well incorporated. Stir in all remaining ingredients, adjusting balance to your own taste. Serve immediately.

Serves 2–3
Preparation time: 10 mins, including 30 mins standing time

Mango Chutney

6 small green mangoes, peeled, halved and stone removed
6 dried chillies, soaked until soft
4 tablespoons oil
2 teaspoons salt
2 tablespoons finely chopped ginger
1 teaspoon *garam masala*
2 tablespoons raisins or sultanas
250 ml (1 cup) vinegar
60 ml (1/4 cup) water
2 teaspoons ground cumin, or cumin seeds
8 cloves garlic, thinly sliced
90 g (3 oz) brown or demerara sugar

1 Cut each mango half into two pieces lengthwise, then again crosswise, so each half yields four pieces.
2 Drain chilies and pat dry. Heat oil in a wok over medium heat and fry chilies for about 45 seconds, until almost brown and slightly puffy. Add salt, ginger, and *garam masala* and stir for about 2 minutes over low heat. Add mangoes and remaining ingredients and cook for 8 to 10 minutes or until mango is tender but not mushy.
3 Let chutney cool before transferring to a clean glass jar. Cover tightly and refrigerate for at least one day (preferably three to four days) before eating.

Makes 1 large jar chutney
Cooking time: 13 mins
Preparation time: 15 mins

Pickled Green Chilies

20 fat green chilies, washed, stalks discarded
500 ml (2 cups) distilled white vinegar
1/2 teaspoon salt
2 teaspoons sugar

1 Slice chilies diagonally, about 5 mm (1/5 in) thick.
2 Bring vinegar to a boil with salt and sugar over high heat. Add chilies and simmer for 15 seconds. Pour all into a clean screwtop jar. Once cool, cover, and store in the fridge.

Makes 1 large jar pickled chilies
Cooking time: 3 mins
Preparation time: 10 mins

Cucumber Raita Indian Yoghurt Relish

There are countless Indian *raita*s, all based on the combination of vegetables and yoghurt. Here, cucumber amplifies the dish's cooling character.

1 cucumber
1 small red onion, peeled and sliced into thin rings
2 teaspoons salt
250 g (9 oz) thick plain yoghurt
1 tablespoon lime juice

1 Peel cucumber and quarter it lengthwise, then slice into thin quarter-moons. Mix with onion rings and sprinkle with salt. Set aside for 20 minutes, then drain, squeezing lightly to remove some juice, and rinse well with cold water.
2 Mix vegetables with yoghurt and lime juice. Serve alongside curries and biryanis.

Serves 2–3
Preparation time: 5 mins

Pickled Green Papaya

Crunchy and cool. Equally good paired with spicy curries or cold meats, or eaten neat as a snack.

1 firm green (unripe) papaya, about 650 g (1 1/2 lbs)
2 teaspoons salt
500 ml (2 cups) distilled white vinegar
100 g (3 1/2 oz) caster (superfine) sugar

1 Skin papaya and halve lengthwise. Scrape out white seeds and discard. With a vegetable peeler, shave papaya flesh into long thin strips. Transfer to a large bowl, sprinkle with salt and toss to mix well. Set aside for 40 minutes.
2 Squeeze as much moisture out of papaya as possible. Pack papaya into a large, very clean screwtop jar.
3 Dissolve sugar in vinegar over low heat. Let cool slightly, then pour over papaya. When completely cool, cover tightly. Let steep at least two days before serving. Pickle keeps for a couple of weeks in a cool place.

Makes approximately 600 g (1 lb 5 1/2 oz) pickle
Preparation time: 20 mins, plus 40 mins standing time

Achar   Nonya Vegetable Pickle

A dish that takes some work and time, but that keeps for months in the refrigerator. Sun-dry the vegetables if you can; alternatively, dry them in a low oven.

2 cucumbers
2 carrots
350 g (12^1/$_2$ oz) cabbage
250 g (9 oz) cauliflower
1 tablespoon sea salt
1 liter (4 cups) distilled white vinegar
500 ml (2 cups) water
20 shallots, peeled
20 cloves garlic, peeled
6 tablespoons oil
2 tablespoons sugar
4 tablespoons sesame seeds, lightly toasted
200 g (7 oz) finely chopped roasted
   peanuts

Spice Paste
350 g (12^1/$_2$ oz) onions or shallots
150 g (5^1/$_4$ oz) ginger, peeled
10 dried chilies, soaked till soft
50 g (1^3/$_4$ oz) fresh turmeric, peeled

1 Peel cucumbers and halve lengthwise. Scrape out core, taking care to remove every bit of the soft "jelly," or the cucumber may rot before it dries. Cut cucumber and carrot into thick 5-cm (2-in) lengths, and slice cabbage into 2-cm-wide (1-in) strips. Separate cauliflower into small florets.
2 Spread vegetables out on a large tray and sprinkle with salt. Let stand in the sun for two days, until they are dry to the touch and just slightly shriveled.
3 Bring vinegar and water to the boil in a deep pot. Blanch vegetables, shallots, and garlic cloves, a small batch at a time, until they plump up again — it should take only several seconds per batch. Remove with a slotted spoon and transfer to a clean bowl. There should be very little liquid left at the end.
4 Grind Spice Paste ingredients until fine. Heat oil in a wok over medium heat and fry Spice Paste until fragrant, 7 to 8 minutes. Toss well with remaining blanching liquid, vegetables, sugar, sesame seeds, and peanuts and transfer to two sterilized or very clean, dry screwtop jars. Store in the fridge; let stand at least three days before serving as a side dish.

Makes 1^3/$_4$ kg (4 lbs) pickle
Cooking time: 25 mins
Preparation time: 40 mins, plus drying time

Sambal Blachan with Lime Leaf (see photo on page 25)

The essential Peranakan sambal, without which a Nonya dining table is naked. Sorry, but we think using a food processor for this makes it thoroughly insipid.

1 tablespoon shrimp paste
5 red chilies, finely chopped
3 chili padi, finely chopped
3 lime leaves, central vein discarded and
   very finely shredded
1 tablespoon hot water
3 tablespoons freshly squeezed lime juice

1 Toast shrimp paste over a live flame for about 3 minutes until fragrant, crusty and slightly charred. In a pestle and mortar, grind chilies until fine. Add shrimp paste and pound until incorporated, then add lime leaf and pound to blend. Mix in hot water and lime juice. Serve immediately.

Note To prevent the shrimp paste odor from permeating the house, wrap it in foil and toast in a low oven or in a dry pan for 4 to 5 minutes.

Makes 125 ml (^{1}/$_2$ cup) sambal
Cooking time: 3 mins
Preparation time: 10 mins

Sambal Blachan with Lime Leaf

See recipe on page 22.

Pineapple Relish

2 tablespoons shrimp paste
4 red chilies, finely chopped
2 teaspoons sugar
1 pineapple, about 450 g (1 lb)
1 tablespoon oil

1 Toast shrimp paste over a live flame for 3 minutes (See Sambal Blachan recipe for instructions). Grind hot paste with chilies and sugar until very fine.
2 Skin pineapple and quarter lengthwise. Remove hard core and slice into pieces about 1 cm ($^1/_3$ in) thick.
3 Heat oil in a wok over high heat and fry pineapple slices for 1 to 2 minutes. Remove from heat and chop coarsely. Mix well with shrimp paste and serve immediately.

Makes approximately 500 g (1 lb 2 oz)
Cooking time: 5 mins
Preparation time: 10 mins

Kerabu Timun Cucumber Salad

1 cucumber
$^1/_2$ teaspoon salt
3 tablespoons freshly grated coconut
2 tablespoons freshly squeezed lime juice
1 teaspoon sugar

Spice Paste
2 tablespoons dried shrimp
4 shallots
4 cloves garlic
3 red chilies

1 Soak dried shrimp in warm water until soft, about 40 minutes, then drain and grind with shallots, garlic, and chilies until fine.
2 Peel cucumber and quarter lengthwise. Remove seeds and core, then slice diagonally across into diamond shapes about $^1/_2$ cm ($^1/_4$ in) thick. Sprinkle with salt and set aside.
3 Dry-fry grated coconut in a non-stick frying pan over medium heat for 3 to 5 minutes, stirring constantly, until lightly browned. Drain cucumber of any juices, then toss

with Spice Paste, coconut, lime juice, and sugar. Serve immediately.

Serves 2–3
Cooking time: 5 mins
Preparation time: 10 mins + 40 mins standing time

Sambal Belimbing Starfruit Sambal

200 g (7 oz) belimbing, sliced into thin discs
2 tablespoons salt
6 tablespoons oil
4 cloves garlic, sliced thinly
2 stalks lemongrass, sliced very thinly on the diagonal
150 g ($5^1/_4$ oz) fresh prawns, peeled
250 ml (1 cup) thick coconut milk
2 teaspoons sugar
salt to taste

Spice Paste
1 tablespoon shrimp paste
4 red chilies
150 g ($5^1/_4$ oz) onions

1 Cut each belimbing across into 5-mm-thick ($^1/_4$-in) slices. Sprinkle with salt and set aside for 20 minutes. Very gently squeeze belimbing dry with your hands, transfer to a clean bowl, then rinse well with cold water. Drain again.
2 Grind Spice Paste ingredients until fine. Heat oil in a wok over medium heat. When very hot, fry garlic and lemongrass for 2 to 3 minutes until golden and crispy, then transfer to kitchen paper to drain.
3. In the same oil, fry Spice Paste for 7 to 8 minutes, stirring constantly, until fragrant. Add belimbing, prawns, and coconut milk, bring to a simmer and cook 5 to 6 minutes more until belimbing are soft. Add sugar and salt, garnish with fried lemongrass and garlic and serve with hot rice.

Serves 4–5
Cooking time: 16 mins
Preparation time: 20 mins plus 20 mins standing time

Pickled Radish with Chilies

A typical Cantonese pickle served with roast meats.

1 whole white radish (daikon), about 450 g (1 lb)
3 red chilies
2 teaspoons salt
500 ml (2 cups) distilled white vinegar
75 g (2¹/₂ oz) caster (superfine) sugar

1 Peel radish and cut it into batons the size of a little finger. Slice chilies into large diagonal pieces. Combine both in a bowl and sprinkle with salt. Set aside for 30 mins.
2 Squeeze out and discard as much moisture as possible out of the vegetables, then rinse briefly in cold water and squeeze dry again. Pack into a large, very clean screwtop jar.
3 Bring vinegar and sugar to a boil, then turn off heat and let mixture cool for 5 minutes. Pour over radish and chilies. Let cool completely, then steep overnight, covered, before serving. Pickle keeps for a couple of weeks in a cool place.

Makes approximately 450 g (1 lb) pickle
Cooking time: 1 min
Preparation time: 20 mins, plus 30 mins standing

Chilies, Garlic, and Vinegar

A typical Teochew dip usually served with soy-braised poultry and pork.

6 red chilies
3 cloves garlic, peeled
5 tablespoons distilled white vinegar
¹/₂ teaspoon sugar
¹/₂ teaspoon salt

1 Mince chilies and garlic very fine with a cleaver. Mix with vinegar, sugar and salt. A large batch of this can be made up and kept in a screw-top jar, refrigerated, for a few days.

Serves 3–5
Preparation time: 5 mins

Serondeng Roasted Coconut Sambal

A terribly addictive accompaniment, served as part of an Indonesian *riijstaffel* and also a Nonya long table meal.

200 g (7 oz) freshly grated coconut
3 stalks lemongrass
4 green chilies
6 shallots
³/₄ teaspoon salt

1 Cut off and discard all but the thickest 6 cm (3 in) of each lemongrass stalk. Slice lemongrass, chilies, and shallots finely and toss with coconut to mix.
2 Heat a wok over low flame and dry-fry all ingredients, stirring constantly, until coconut and other ingredients turn an even golden brown, about 10 minutes. Watch mixture diligently to prevent scorching. Cool completely and store airtight in the fridge; eat within a week.

Serves 4–5
Cooking time: 10 mins
Preparation time: 10 mins

Preserved Beancurd, Shallots, and Lime Juice

A typical Chinese side dish eaten with rice porridge. You can also use white fermented beancurd (*foo yee*) which has a slightly milder flavor.

3 squares fermented red beancurd (*lam yee*)
5 shallots, sliced finely
2 tablespoons lime juice
1 teaspoon sugar

1 Lightly mash beancurd until well blended. Gently mix in all remaining ingredients. Serve with porridge or rice and other bland fried dishes.

Serves 2–3
Preparation time: 2 mins

Sambal Goreng Fried Chili Sambal

A basic sambal to serve with meals, especially with dishes like *nasi lemak*, *laksa*, Hokkien mee, and *mee siam*; increase the chilies if you want it hotter. You can use it as a marinade for chicken or seafood — especially prawns and meaty fish — before grilling or barbecuing. And yes, bring it on holiday with you.

6 cloves garlic
4 candlenuts
300 g ($10^1/_2$ oz) large onions
8–10 dried chilies, soaked till soft
2 tablespoons tamarind pulp
200 ml ($^3/_4$ cup plus 1 tablespoon)
** water**
6 tablespoons vegetable oil
2 tablespoons tomato paste
1 teaspoon salt
1 tablespoon sugar

1 Grind garlic, candlenuts, onions and chilies until very fine. If paste is very dry, add a little water to obtain a moist but not soggy texture.
2 Knead tamarind with water until pulp dissolves and strain.
3 Heat oil in a wok over low heat. When very hot, add paste and fry for about 10 minutes, stirring constantly, until paste is thickened and shiny with oil: this indicates the raw spices are adequately cooked.
4 Add tomato paste, salt, sugar, and $^3/_4$ of the tamarind liquid to the wok. Stir well and taste to adjust; add remaining tamarind if necessary. Stir for 1 minute, then scrape into a clean bowl or jar. When cool, cover airtight and store in the fridge. This keeps for a few weeks.

Makes Approximately 500 g (1 lb 2 oz) sambal
Cooking time: 12 mins
Preparation time: 10 mins

Sambal Ikan Bilis   Crispy Anchovies and Peanut

oil for deep-frying
6 tablespoons raw red-skinned peanuts
200 g (7 oz) dried *ikan bilis*, cleaned
1 tablespoon tamarind pulp
4 tablespoons water
4 tablespoons oil
1/4 teaspoon salt
1 tablespoon sugar
1 tablespoon tomato paste

Spice Paste
3 red chilies
200 g (7 oz) onion, sliced
4 cloves garlic
1 teaspoon shrimp paste

Serves 4–6
Cooking time: 16 mins
Preparation time: 20 mins

1 Heat oil in a wok over medium-low heat until it ripples under the surface, but there is no haze, about 140°C (275°F). Add peanuts and fry, stirring frequently, for about 4 minutes or until golden (scrape skin off one to check). Remove from oil with a slotted spoon and drain on kitchen paper.
2 Spread *ikan bilis* on a plate and microwave on high for 1$^1/_2$ minutes to make sure it is very dry. (Alternatively, sun it for a while.) Return oil to frying temperature, add *ikan bilis* and fry for 4 to 5 minutes or until crisp and golden brown. Drain well on kitchen paper. Discard oil
3 Grind Spice Paste ingredients until fine. Knead tamarind with water until pulp dissolves, then strain.
4 Heat 4 tablespoons fresh oil in a clean wok over medium-high heat and fry spice paste for 6 minutes, until fragrant and thickened. Add tamarind liquid, salt, sugar, and tomato paste and stir to blend well. Bring to a quick boil, add *ikan bilis* and peanuts and mix well, then dish up.

Brinjal Sambal Eggplant Sambal

Brinjals (or eggplants or aubergines) come in all shapes and sizes. The most typically Singaporean ones are the slim purple brinjals about 30 cm (1 ft) long, though the short Japanese ones about 12 cm (5 in) long and the fat, black-purple ones more common in the West can be used here too.

1 tablespoon tamarind pulp
4 tablespoons water
6 tablespoons oil
$1/_3$ teaspoon salt
1 tablespoon sugar
1 tablespoon tomato paste
2 slim purple brinjals, or 5 small
  Japanese eggplants

Spice Paste
6 dried red chilies, soaked until soft
1 large onion
6 cloves garlic
1 tablespoon shrimp paste

1 Knead tamarind with water until pulp dissolves, then strain. Grind Spice Paste ingredients until fine.
2 Heat oil a in a wok over medium heat. Fry Spice Paste for 5 to 6 minutes or until fragrant, then add tamarind liquid, salt, sugar, and tomato paste and cook for 1 minute more. Keep Sambal warm.
3 Halve brinjals lengthways. If using big ones, cut each half into three pieces. Cook brinjals as desired (see Note). Pour sambal over brinjals and serve hot.

Note   Brinjals are tastiest flash-deep-fried in hot oil until tender, but also greasy. You can pan-fry them with a little oil in a non-stick pan over high heat, turning frequently, or blanch or steam them for 2 to 3 minutes, until soft.

Serves 2–3
Cooking time: 10 mins
Preparation time: 10 mins

Sambal Fish

A delicious home-style Malay dish that needs nothing but hot white rice and sliced cucumber on the side.

600 g (1 lb 5$^1/_2$ oz) meaty fish, cut into
  thick steaks or slices
oil for deep-frying
1 tablespoon tamarind pulp
2 tablespoons water
1 tablespoon tomato puree
1 teaspoon sugar
1 teaspoon salt
juice of 2 limes
sliced cucumber, for garnish

Sambal Paste
1 large onion
4 cloves garlic
1 tablespoon shrimp paste
8 dried chilies, soaked till soft

1 Heat oil and fry fish until crisp and golden brown. Set aside to keep warm.
2 Knead tamarind with water until pulp dissolves, then strain. Grind Spice Paste ingredients until fine. Remove all but 4 tablespoons of oil and fry paste over medium heat for 6 to 8 minutes. Add tamarind liquid, tomato puree, sugar and salt and stir for 2 minutes.
3 Add fish to paste and stir well to incorporate. Dribble lime juices all over before serving with sliced cucumber.

Serves 4
Cooking time: 20 minutes

Prawn Sambal

A tasty dish simple enough for everyday — or fancy enough for occasions, if you use large, fresh tiger prawns. Leave their shells and heads on for a more flavorful gravy.

1¹/₂ tablespoons tamarind pulp
3 tablespoons water
6 tablespoons vegetable oil
2 teaspoons sugar
2 tablespoons tomato paste
¹/₂ teaspoon salt
500 g (1 lb 2 oz) medium-sized prawns, shelled
200 g (7 oz) *buah petai* (optional)

Spice Paste
6 dried chilies, soaked until soft
350 g (12¹/₂ oz) onion, sliced
5 cloves garlic
1 tablespoon shrimp paste

1 Knead tamarind with water until pulp dissolves, then strain. Grind Spice Paste ingredients until fine.
2 Heat oil in a wok over medium heat and fry Spice Paste for 6 to 8 minutes until fragrant and thickened. Add tamarind liquid, sugar, tomato paste, and salt and bring to a boil.
3 Add prawns and *petai*, if using, and fry for 2 to 3 minutes or until prawns are cooked through. Serve hot.

Note Petai are small, vivid green beans similar in size to broad beans, with a faintly sulphurous flavor that is something of an acquired taste.

Serves 4
Cooking time: 12 mins
Preparation time: 15 mins

Grilled Stingray with Sambal

Known as skate in the West, stingray is a meaty, succulent fish excellent for grilling or barbecuing. This recipe works with other firm-textured fish, such as shark or swordfish. Add some oil to the rub if the fish is very lean.

600 g (1 lb 5¹/₂ oz) stingray, skin removed
2 tablespoons *ketjap manis* **or thick dark soy sauce**
1 tablespoon freshly-ground black pepper
¹/₂ teaspoon salt
1 teaspoon sugar
cut limes and chili sauce or Sambal Goreng (p. 28), to serve

1 Wash stingray well and pat dry. Mix *ketjap manis*, pepper, salt, and sugar together and rub over stingray.
2 Grill stingray under a hot grill or over hot coals, turning once, for 4 to 5 minutes per side, or until cooked through. Serve hot with cut limes and chili sauce or Sambal Goreng on the side.

Serves 2–3
Cooking time: 10 mins
Preparation time: 5 mins

Entertaining Snacks

Actually, we believe that any item of good food is an excuse for a party, but here are some recipes that we have found go down especially well with a crowd.

Jaganan Vegetable Salad with Peanut Sauce

A mysteriously-named dish clearly related to the very similar Indonesian Gado Gado — but which derives from which? No matter, both are delicious.

3 tablespoons vegetable oil
2 firm beancurd cakes (*tau kwa*)
$^1/_4$ white cabbage
10 long beans
625 ml (2$^1/_2$ cups) water
150 g (5$^1/_4$ oz) beansprouts
1 cucumber, sliced thinly
4 hard-boiled eggs, sliced thinly
prawn crackers for garnish

Sauce
10 dried chilies, soaked till soft
1 tablespoon shrimp paste
150 g (5$^1/_4$ oz) onion, sliced
4 cloves garlic
2 tablespoons tamarind pulp
600 ml (2$^1/_2$ cups) water
$^1/_4$ teaspoon salt
1 tablespoon palm or brown sugar
4 tablespoons ground roasted peanuts

Serves 4–6
Cooking time: 20 mins
Preparation time: 20 mins

1 To make Sauce, grind chilies, shrimp paste, onion, and garlic until fine. Knead tamarind with water until pulp dissolves, then strain into a non-metallic pot. Bring to a boil over medium heat, then add spice paste, salt, and sugar and simmer, stirring, for 3 to 4 minutes or until aromatic. Stir in ground peanuts. The Sauce should be thick; if not, cook down a little more. Let cool.
2 Heat oil in a wok or frying pan over high heat and fry beancurd cakes until browned on all sides, 5 to 6 minutes. Let cool and slice into thin pieces.
3 Wash and cut cabbage and long beans into bite-sized pieces. Boil a large pot of water and blanch both vegetables in batches until just tender, 1 to 2 minutes per batch. Blanch beansprouts for 30 seconds.
4 Arrange all vegetables, hard-boiled eggs, beancurd cake, and prawn crackers on serving platter. Serve Sauce separately for diners to help themselves to.

Note Other vegetables that could be added to the line-up include blanched kangkong (water convolvulus), cubed boiled potatoes, French beans (see picture below), and perhaps even asparagus.

Choose very fresh, firm French beans.

Bergedel Potato and Fish Cakes

The Dutch colonization of Indonesia birthed many a fascinating hybrid dish. Danish *frikadeller* meatballs were transformed into bergedel, minced meat and potato balls now an essential part of any *nasi padang* (rice and cooked food) stall's repertoire. Terry's version uses fish, which makes them similar to the fish cutlets of Sri Lanka, itself once colonized by the Portuguese … but that's another story.

750 g (1 lb 11 oz) potatoes
3 tablespoons oil
2 tablespoons chopped onion
1 tablespoon ground garlic
250 g (9 oz) flaked cooked fish
1 teaspoon freshly ground black pepper
1 teaspoon salt
1/2 teaspoon ground cloves
4 tablespoons plain flour
2 eggs, beaten to blend
oil for deep-frying

Serves 6–8
Cooking time: 45 mins
Preparation time: 20 mins

1 Cook potatoes in boiling water for 16 to 20 minutes (or microwave on High) until soft. Drain very well and peel, then mash fine.
2 Heat oil in a wok over medium heat and fry onion and garlic for 5 to 6 minutes or until softened and lightly browned. Mix with mash, fish, pepper, salt, and cloves until well blended.
3 Heat oil in a wok over medium heat. With well-floured hands, roll egg-sized balls of mash into flat patties. Dust each bergedel lightly with flour, then coat well with the beaten egg and slip into the hot oil. Deep-fry in batches, for 3 to 5 minutes per batch, turning once, until golden brown. Drain well on kitchen paper and serve hot.

Note You can use any white fish — even drained canned water-packed tuna, in a pinch.

An imperial version of the slightly more plebeian *won ton*, served as a snack or side dish by hawkers. *Sui kow* skins are circular, as opposed to square *won ton* skins.

1200 ml (1¼ cups) water
2 tablespoons *ikan bilis*
200 g (7 oz) minced pork
150 g (5¼ oz) minced prawns
150 g (5¼ oz) crab meat
2 stalks spring onions, chopped
4 tablespoons light soy sauce
1 tablespoon cornflour
1 teaspoon white or black pepper
1½ teaspoons sesame oil
20–25 *sui gow* skins
1 teaspoon cornstarch mixed with 1 table-
spoon water

Serves 5–6
Cooking time: 30 mins
Preparation time: 20 mins

1 Bring water to the boil, add *ikan bilis* and simmer for 15 minutes. Strain stock and discard *ikan bilis*.

2 Mix minced pork, prawns, crab meat, spring onions, 1 tablespoon light soy sauce, cornflour, pepper, and half the sesame oil together until well blended. Place 1 heaped teaspoon of filling on a *sui gow* skin, fold over to make a half-moon shape, and seal edges with a little cornstarch slurry. Repeat with remaining skins and filling.

3 Bring a large pot of water to the boil. Slip in half the *sui gow* and simmer for 5 to 6 minutes until they float up. Drain and transfer to stock pot. Repeat with remaining *sui gow*.

4 Add remaining soy sauce and sesame oil to stock and reheat all until just about to boil. Serve immediately.

Crab Cakes

Toothsome little morsels quite different from their American cousins.

650 g (1 lb 7 oz) cooked crab meat
2 lime leaves, sliced hair thin
2 eggs, lightly beaten
$1/_2$ teaspoon sea salt
3 tablespoons plain flour
Oil for deep-frying
sliced cucumber, for garnish
chili sauce, to serve

Spice Paste
100 g ($3^1/_2$ oz) onions
6 dried chilies, soaked until soft
1 tablespoon ground coriander
1 teaspoon shrimp paste
1 stalk lemongrass

1 Grind Spice Paste ingredients until very fine.
2 Mix Spice Paste, crab meat, lime leaves, beaten egg, salt, and flour together until well blended. Scoop heaped tablespoons of mixture and pat into small cakes about 1 cm ($1/_2$ in) thick.
3 Heat oil in a wok over medium heat until shimmering. Deep-fry cakes in batches until golden brown, 2 to 3 minutes per batch, turning once. Drain on kitchen paper and serve with sliced cucumber and chili sauce.

Serves 6–8
Cooking time: 6–10 minutes
Preparation time: 15 minutes

Ngoh Hiang   Pork, Prawn, and Crab Rolls

Peranakans, Teochews, and Hokkiens all have their own spins on this deep-fried meat roll. We say *vive la différence*.

200 g (7 oz) shelled prawns
400 g (14$^1/_4$ oz) minced pork
6 water chestnuts, peeled and finely diced
1 clove garlic, very finely chopped
2 shallots, very finely chopped
2 teaspoons rice wine
1 teaspoon light soy sauce
$^1/_2$ teaspoon sugar
$^3/_4$ teaspoon salt
150 g (5$^1/_4$ oz) cooked crabmeat
2 sheets beancurd skin
1 tablespoon cornstarch, dissolved in
   1 tablespoon water
sweet flour sauce and chili sauce, to serve

Serves 6–8
Cooking time: 20 mins
Preparation time: 20 mins

1 Using a Chinese cleaver, chop prawns until coarsely minced. Mix prawns with pork, water chestnuts, garlic, and shallots until well blended, then sprinkle over rice wine, soy sauce, sugar, and salt and mix well. Gently mix in crabmeat and set aside.

2 Trim off thick edges of beancurd skin. Cut sheets into six 23 cm x 30 cm (9 in x 12 in) rectangles and rinse quickly under running water to remove excess oil and salt. Gently pat dry.

3 Lay a rectangle flat on a work surface. Place 3 tablespoons of filling along a short side and pat it into a log shape, leaving small margins at each end. Roll skin around the filling, tucking in the sides as you go. Smear a little cornstarch solution along seam and press to seal. Repeat with remaining skin and filling.

4 Place rolls in a lightly greased steamer tray, spacing at least 1 cm ($^1/_2$ in) apart. Steam over high heat for 9 minutes, or until just cooked. Transfer rolls to a lightly oiled plate and let cool.

5 Heat oil in a wok until very hot and just starting to haze. Fry *ngoh hiang* in 3 or 4 batches; carefully lower rolls into oil and fry, turning occasionally, until golden brown all over. Drain *ngoh hiang* on paper towels and slice diagonally into bite-size pieces. Serve with sweet flour sauce and chili sauce for dipping.

Otak Otak Spicy Fish Pâté Grilled in Banana Leaves

An intoxicating blend of fish, spices, fragrant herbs and a touch of char from the grill. Eat with *nasi lemak*, or make sandwiches with it on buttered crusty bread.

3 lime leaves, sliced hair thin
small handful laksa leaves (*daun kesom*), sliced
1 teaspoon salt
1 teaspoon sugar
750 g (1 lb 11 oz) deboned mackerel meat
3 eggs, lightly beaten
2 tablespoons oil
200 ml (³/₄ cup plus 1 tablespoon) thick coconut milk
6–8 squares of banana leaf, each about 25 cm (10 in) across

Spice Paste
300 g (10¹/₂ oz) onions
8 candlenuts
12 dried chilies, soaked until soft
2 tablespoons ground coriander
1 tablespoon shrimp paste
3 slices galangal
2 stalks lemongrass

1 Grind Spice Paste ingredients until fine. Mix with lime leaves and laksa leaves, salt and sugar.
2 Grind fish meat in a food processor to a slightly coarse paste. Transfer to a bowl and add eggs, oil, and Spice Paste. Stir with a spoon in one direction only. Slowly mix in coconut milk. The finished paste should have a consistency like softened butter.
3 Scald banana leaves in boiling water to soften, and drain. Place 2 to 3 tablespoons of fish mixture in the centre of each square, spreading it about 6 mm (¹/₄ in) thick, and fold opposite edges over to enclose. Secure the ends with toothpicks, weaving them through the leaf layers (as you would pin pieces of fabric together).
4 Cook under a hot grill or over charcoal for 8 to 10 minutes, turning once half way through. Serve hot, and unwrap at table.

Note An oily fish is needed to stand up to the spices. Chris has made this with a mix of trout and mackerel, cutting back on the spice paste slightly, with great success.

Serves 4–5
Cooking time: 10 mins
Preparation time: 25 mins

Mix in coconut milk slowly, stirring until the mixture becomes smooth.

Spread about 3 tablespoons of paste in the middle of each leaf square.

Fold one edge over paste, then opposite edge over that.

Sambal Roast Chicken

The chicken is twice cooked, first in a rich coconut milk gravy, whose spices recall satay marinade, and then grilled to crisp the skin. You can make it with small chicken portions or spring chickens (Cornish Game hens) too.

4 tablespoons vegetable oil
1 chicken, split in half
440 ml (1³/₄ cups) coconut milk
6 lime leaves
2 stalks lemongrass, bruised
1 teaspoon salt
1 tablespoon palm or brown sugar
4 slices galangal

Spice Paste
2¹/₂ tablespoons finely chopped onions
1 tablespoon minced ginger
3 cloves garlic
4 dried chilies, soaked till soft
2 tablespoons ground coriander
1 tablespoon ground cumin
1 teaspoon ground fennel

1 Grind Spice Paste ingredients until fine. Heat oil in wok over medium heat and fry spice paste for 5 minutes, or until fragrant and thickened.
2 Add coconut milk, lime leaves, lemongrass, salt, sugar, and galangal and stir well, then add chicken and bring to the boil. Simmer for 40 minutes, partially covered, turning chicken a few times, until bird is cooked through but not falling apart, and gravy is thick.
3 Transfer chicken to a roasting or grill pan. Make several deep gashes over thickest parts of chicken and dribble sauce liberally all over. Grill under high heat for 10 to 15 minutes, turning a few times and basting frequently with the sauce to build up a good crust, until browned all over. Serve with remaining sauce (reduce it a bit over high heat if desired) on the side.

Serves 4
Cooking time: 1 hour
Preparation time: 15 mins

Curry Puffs

Old-fashioned Indian Muslim-style curry puffs used to be shaped out of hand-made puff pastry, rich with margarine, and baked in diesel-fired clay ovens. Commercial butter puff pastry is much more convenient and less laden with hydrogenated fat.

5 tablespoons oil
225 g (8 oz) minced mutton or beef
3 large potatoes, cooked, peeled and diced
250 ml (1 cup) water
1 teaspoon salt
900 g (2 lbs) ready-made butter puff
   pastry
2 hard-boiled eggs, chunkily diced
2 eggs, beaten

Spice Paste
3 tablespoons Meat Curry Powder (p. 17)
1 onion, sliced
5 cloves garlic
2 tablespoons chopped ginger
4 dried chilies, soaked till soft
1 tablespoon water

1 Grind Spice Paste ingredients together until very fine.
2 Heat oil in a wok over medium heat and fry Spice Paste until fragrant and thickened, 5 to 6 minutes. Add beef and fry 2 minutes, then add potatoes, water, and salt. Cook, stirring frequently, until liquid has largely evaporated and curry is thick, 6 to 7 minutes. Let cool completely.
3 Roll out puff pastry 3 mm ($1/8$ in) thick. Cut into 15-cm (6-in) squares. Place a heaped tablespoon of filling across a diagonal half of a square, and top with some boiled egg pieces. Fold over pastry to make a triangle and seal edges with some beaten egg. Brush top with more beaten egg to glaze. Repeat with remaining pastries and filling.
4 Transfer curry puffs to a parchment-lined baking sheet and bake in a preheated oven at 200°C (400°F) for 10 to 12 minutes or until well browned. Serve warm.

Makes 8–9 curry puffs
Cooking time: 25 mins
Preparation time: 30 mins

Sardine Puffs

Another slightly retro party standby. Who would have thought canned fish could be so perked up by chilies, onions and lime?

425 g (15 oz) canned sardines
2 tablespoons water
3 tablespoons ketchup
1 tablespoon freshly squeezed lime juice
$1/2$ teaspoon sugar
$1/4$ teaspoon salt
1 tablespoon oil
1 large onion, chopped
3 red chilies, thinly sliced
700 g (1 lb 9 oz) butter puff pastry
2 hard-boiled eggs, sliced
1 egg, beaten

Makes 7–8 puffs
Cooking time: 18 mins
Preparation time: 25 mins

1 Lift sardines out of the tomato sauce in the can. Remove spine bones. Add water, ketchup, lime juice, sugar, and salt to tomato sauce in can and stir to mix.
2 Heat oil in a wok over medium-high heat. Fry onion and chili until softened, 3 to 4 minutes, then add contents of can. Cook 1 to 2 minutes, stirring constantly, until thickened, then add sardines. Stir gently to break up flesh into large flakes. Scrape into a bowl and set aside to cool for a while.
3 Roll out pastry and make puffs as for Curry Puffs (above). Place puffs on a parchment-lined baking sheet and bake in a preheated oven at 200°C (400°F) for 10 to 12 minutes or until well browned. Serve warm.

Note For a speedier version, mix sardines straight from the can with 2 to 3 tablespoons of Sambal Goreng (p. 28), thinly sliced raw shallots and a squeeze of lime juice, then make the puffs.

Roti John · Fried Bread with Mutton and Egg

A throwback to colonial days, endowed with an Anglo-Saxon name in honor of the foreign bread it's made with! Made at home, this is much less oily and fresher-tasting than most hawker versions.

250 g (9 oz) minced lamb or mutton
1 large onion, chopped
2 cloves garlic, finely minced
4 tablespoons chopped fresh coriander
1/2 teaspoon ground cloves
3/4 teaspoon ground cinnamon
1/2 teaspoon ground nutmeg
3/4 teaspoon black pepper
1 teaspoon salt
1 medium baguette-type loaf (such as
   a *bâtard*)
5 eggs
2 tablespoons oil
chili sauce and sliced tomato and cucumber,
   to serve

1 Mix mutton with onion, garlic, coriander, cloves, cinnamon, nutmeg, black pepper, and salt. Refrigerate 1 hour. Cut loaf into half horizontally, then cut each half into 3 or 4 pieces. Set aside, uncovered, to dry out slightly.
2 Beat 2 eggs and set aside. Crack remaining 3 eggs into meat mixture and mix loosely — it should be sloppy and uneven in texture.
3 Lightly grease a large frying pan with a little of the oil and set over medium-low heat. Brush cut sides of a bread piece with some of the beaten egg, then spoon a layer of meat mixture over, pressing gently to smooth and compact it. Add to pan face down and fry for 8 to 10 minutes, turning after 5 minutes, until meat is browned and bread is crisp. Repeat with remaining bread and meat mixture. Do not crowd pan; fry in 2 or 3 batches.
4 Serve hot with chili sauce, tomato, and cucumber.

Serves 4–5
Prep time: 15 min + 1 hour marinating time
Cooking time: 20 min

Hawker Favourites

The hawkers of the post-war period were itinerant food vendors, many of whom operated out of make-shift carts, lean-tos and baskets slung on poles. Terry remembers bleary-eyed nights of his youth, when the prospect of earning $2 per night, plus all the noodles he could eat, led him to work for the *mee pok* (noodles) man, walking round the neighbourhood click-clacking two bamboo clappers to announce the hawker's arrival, taking orders, and delivering scalding hot bowls on wooden trays. Alas, today many hawker stalls and specialties — and more importantly, the experience and skill that went into the food preparation — have vanished. The modern air-conditioned food courts, while hygienic and cool, do not have an ounce of the ambience of the old open-air hawker venues, such as those at Somerset and Chinatown, or the former Satay Club at Beach Road. Here are some of the classic hawker favourites that we make at home.

Roti Prata Crispy Pan-fried Bread

Distinctly different from the true Indian *paratha* of wholewheat flour, this is a multilayered pan-fried bread also known as *roti chanai* in Malaysia. Hawkers flip the dough, whirling it through the air until it is tissue-thin, but for the novice it is easier to stretch it as described here, rather like strudel dough.

500 g (1 lb 2 oz) plain flour, sifted
1 teaspoon salt
1 teaspoon sugar
125 ml ($^1/_2$ cup) lukewarm water
4 tablespoons lukewarm milk
150 g (5$^1/_4$ oz) vegetable ghee or
  melted margarine
vegetable or meat curry gravy, to serve

Makes about 12–14 prata
Cooking time: 4 mins per *prata*
Preparation time: 40 mins + 45 mins standing
  time

1 Combine flour, salt, and sugar in a mixing bowl. Mix in water, milk, and 2 tablespoons of the margarine with your hands and knead gently but constantly for about 7 minutes, adding more water or flour as necessary for a soft, coherent dough. Pinch off pieces the size of large plums and shape into balls. Roll balls in remaining margarine to coat and place on a plate. Cover with plastic wrap and let stand in a cool place for 45 minutes.
2 Have a frying pan, preferably non-stick, at the ready over medium-high heat.
3 Lightly grease a worksurface or large chopping board. Place a dough ball on it and dab with a bit more melted margarine. Flatten lightly with your fingers, then stretch dough outwards, working from the center all the way to the edge and moving clockwise or anticlockwise around the circle. Try to make dough as evenly thin as you can.
4 Fold two opposite edges to the center and then the other two edges, to make a rough square. Drop *prata* into pan, folded side downwards, and fry for 2 to 3 minutes or until underside is browned. Flip *prata* and fry to brown other side, 2 minutes more. Transfer to a plate. Repeat with remaining dough balls.
5 Just before serving *prata*, stack them and clap them very quickly between your hands so they crumple up. They will spring back into shape, but their internal layers will now be fluffed up. Serve with plenty of curry gravy on the side.

Note Crack an egg onto the stretched dough and smear it out a bit before folding and frying. Large *pratas* folded around minced meat, onion and egg before frying are called *murtabaks*.

Stretch the dough as thin as you can.

Fold two opposite edges to the center ...

... and then the other two edges, to make a rough square.

Nasi Goreng Malay-style Fried Rice

A spicy Malay version of basic fried rice. Add color and crunch with diced vegetables of your choice.

4 tablespoons vegetable oil
600 g (1 lb 5$^1/_2$ oz) cold, cooked rice
200 g (7 oz) cooked, shredded chicken
$^3/_4$ teaspoon salt
3 eggs
sliced cucumber and Sambal Goreng
  (p. 25), to serve

Spice Paste
3 red chilies
8 shallots
4 cloves garlic
1 tablespoon shrimp paste
1 tablespoon dried shrimp, soaked
  until soft

1 Grind Spice Paste ingredients fine. Heat oil in a wok over medium-high heat and fry paste for 4 to 5 minutes until fragrant. Add cold rice, chicken, and salt and toss well for 1 to 2 minutes to coat grains evenly with spices and heat them through.
2 Push rice aside to make a well and crack eggs into it. Scramble until softly set, then toss with rice to mix. Serve with sliced cucumber and Sambal Goreng on the side.

Serves 2–3
Cooking time: 8 mins
Preparation time: 15 mins

Nasi Lemak   Fragrant Coconut Rice

Soothingly rich rice meant to be accompanied by side dishes and sambals of contrasting textures, of which the must-haves are sliced cucumber, Sambal Goreng (p. 25), Sambal Ikan Bilis (p. 29), a fried egg, and a small whole fish, rubbed with salt and deep-fried to a crisp. Pad it out with fried chicken wings or drumsticks, a sambal vegetable and perhaps some *achar* on the side.

300 g (10^1/$_2$ oz) jasmine or long-grain
  uncooked rice
250 ml (1 cup) thick coconut milk
250 ml (1 cup) water
2 pandan leaves, knotted
1^1/$_2$ teaspoons salt

Serves 3–4
Cooking time: 30 mins
Preparation time: 10 mins + 30 mins
  standing time

1 Wash rice well until water runs virtually clear. Drain well. Combine rice, coconut milk, water, and pandan leaves in a rice cooker pot and mix well. Set aside to soak for 30 minutes.
2 Stir in salt and switch rice cooker on. When done, fluff with a fork and serve hot.
3 Alternatively, bring rice to the boil in a heavy-based pot (coconut milk scorches easily), then reduce heat to very low and cook, tightly covered, 20 to 25 minutes or until done.

Note The more recently rice has been harvested, the less water it needs to cook. When cooking rice, it is better to err on the side of caution with the liquid — you can always add a little bit more water as the rice cooks, but you can do little to revive soggy rice.

Hainanese Chicken Rice

You know a dish deserves ambassadorial status when it appears on a Singapore Airlines menu. Originating from Hainan Island, this was made with a particular breed of chicken, with yellow fat and flavorful flesh, from Wenchang province. The chili sauce is a purely Singaporean addition.

1 large chicken
2¹/₂ liters (10 cups) water
3 cloves garlic, peeled
2 slices of ginger
thick black soy sauce, fresh coriander sprigs, cucumber slices, spring onions, to serve

Rice
600 g (1 lb 5¹/₂ oz) uncooked rice
2 tablespoons finely chopped garlic
1¹/₂ tablespoons finely chopped ginger
1 tablespoon finely chopped shallot
2 pandan leaves, tied in a loose knot
2 teaspoons salt, or to taste

Chili Sauce
6 large red chilies
3–5 chili padi
2 large cloves garlic
2 teaspoons minced ginger
¹/₂ teaspoon sugar
¹/₂ teaspoon salt, or to taste
2 tablespoons freshly-squeezed calamansi lime juice

Ginger Sauce
100 g (3¹/₂ oz) old ginger, peeled and sliced
1 tablespoon oil

1 Clean chicken thoroughly. Remove excess fat and reserve. In a large, deep pot, bring water to a rolling boil. Fully submerge chicken in water and return it to a rolling boil. Simmer vigorously, partially covered, for 15 minutes, then cover tightly, switch off heat and let stand 20 minutes.
2 Wash rice well and drain, then spread out on a large plate and let it dry, 10 to 15 minutes. Chop reserved chicken fat into small pieces. Combine with 2 tablespoons cold water in a small pot and cook over low heat for 10 to 15 minutes, until water is evaporated and fat has rendered.
3 Remove chicken from hot stock. Rub skin with sesame oil and set aside.
4 To make Rice, heat 5 tablespoons rendered chicken fat in a wok over medium heat. Fry garlic, ginger, and shallot until fragrant, 1 to 2 minutes. Add rice and stir-fry gently 2 to 3 minutes or until grains turn translucent. Transfer rice to rice cooker, add pandan leaves, salt and 750 ml (3 cups) of the stock from the chicken pot. Switch on and leave to cook.
5 To make Chili Sauce, blend all ingredients to a paste, then add 2 tablespoons hot stock and blend until combined. To make Ginger Sauce, blend ginger to a paste, then add oil and 1 tablespoon hot chicken stock and blend until combined.
6 Chop chicken into pieces before serving with rice, sauces, and garnishes. Serve any remaining chicken stock as soup.

Serves 4–6
Cooking time: 45 mins
Preparation time: 30 mins

Gently immerse the chicken in the boiling water.

Fry the washed, drained rice until the grains turn translucent.

Mee Goreng   Spicy Fried Yellow Noodles

One of the very few noodle dishes in the pantheon of Singapore Indian dishes, a spicy take off of stir-fried Chinese noodles. (See Sambal Goreng, p. 25.)

3 tablespoons vegetable oil
2 cloves garlic, crushed
150 g (5$^1/_4$ oz) fresh prawns, shelled
500 g (1 lb 2 oz) fresh yellow wheat
  noodles
75 g (2$^3/_4$ oz) beansprouts
100 g (3$^1/_2$ oz) choy sum, separated into
  individual leaves
3 tablespoons water
4 tablespoons Sambal Goreng (p. 25)
1 potato, boiled, peeled, and diced
2 tomatoes, quartered
1 teaspoon salt, or to taste
3 eggs

1 Heat oil in a wok over high heat and fry garlic for 1 minute, until golden and fragrant. Add prawns, noodles, beansprouts, and choy sum and fry for 2 minutes.
2 Add water, Sambal Goreng, potato, tomatoes, and salt and stir vigorously for 2 minutes. Push noodles to one side, crack eggs into wok and scramble until just set, 1 to 2 minutes. Toss well to mix. Serve hot.

Note Instead of prawns, you can use sliced fish cake or shredded, boiled chicken or mutton.

Serves 3–4
Cooking time: 7 mins
Preparation time: 15 mins

Bee Hoon Goreng Indian-Muslim Fried Rice Noodles

150 g (5¹/₄ oz) dried *bee hoon*
  (rice vermicelli)
3 chicken thighs, cut into small pieces
¹/₂ teaspoon ground cumin
¹/₂ teaspoon ground coriander
¹/₄ teaspoon ground cinnamon
¹/₄ teaspoon ground turmeric
4 cloves garlic, finely chopped
2–3 tablespoons hot chili sauce
2–3 tablespoons ketchup
1 tablespoon light soy sauce
2 teaspoons sugar, or to taste
1 teaspoon salt, or to taste
4 tablespoons water
5 tablespoons oil
1 large onion, sliced
20 curry leaves
5 white cabbage leaves, finely shredded
3 green chilies, sliced thickly
3 eggs

1 Soak *bee hoon* in cold water for 15 minutes or until softened but not soggy. Drain well. Cut into 10-cm (4-in) hanks.
2 Mix chicken with ground spices and garlic and let marinate 15 minutes, six ingredients together and set aside.
3 Heat oil in a wok over medium-high heat. Add onion and fry 2 minutes, then add curry leaves, cabbage, chilies, and chicken and fry for 3 to 4 minutes or until chicken is just cooked through.
4 Add *bee hoon* and stir for 1 minute, then add sauce mixture and fry vigorously for 2 to 3 minutes. Push *beehoon* to one side, crack eggs into wok and scramble until just set. Stir to mix all well, and serve immediately.

Serves 2–3
Cooking time: 10 mins
Preparation time: 15 mins + 15 mins standing time

Char Kway Teow   Fried Rice Noodles

One of those dishes that inspires fanatical allegiance to a stall that gets it right. What made it memorable in days of yore was lashings of lard and pork cracklings (*chee yow char*) and fat blood cockles (*see hum*). These days, health-conscious diners eschew one or both of these, and recent years have seen new versions of *char kway teow* topped with mounds of steamed greens and crispy *ikan bilis* (whitebait).

4 tablespoons lard or vegetable oil
1¹/₂ tablespoons crushed garlic
1 Chinese sausage, very thinly sliced
150 g (5¹/₄ oz) fish cake, sliced thinly
1 small squid, cleaned and head discarded, sliced into rings and tentacle clumps
150 g (5¹/₄ oz) fresh prawns, peeled
350 g (12¹/₂ oz) *kway teow* (fresh rice noodles)
75 g (2³/₄ oz) beansprouts
3 eggs
3 tablespoons *ketjap manis* or thick dark sweet soy sauce
1 teaspoon light soy sauce
1–2 tablespoons chili sauce
3 tablespoons water

1 Heat lard or oil in a wok over high heat and fry garlic for 1 minute, until golden and fragrant. Add Chinese sausage, fish cake, squid, and prawns and stir-fry for 2 minutes.
2 Add beansprouts, *kway teow*, soy sauces, and chili sauce and stir vigorously for 3 to 4 minutes until well mixed. Noodles should be moist and aromatic. Taste and adjust seasoning if necessary and serve hot.

Note If you can get fresh shelled blood cockles, then add as many of them as you like half-way through step 2. They should be just barely cooked when the noodles are ready. If you cannot get thick dark sweet soy sauce, substitute 2 tablespoons thick dark soy sauce or normal dark soy sauce, mixed with 1 tablespoon brown sugar.

Serves 3–4
Cooking time: 5 mins
Preparation time: 15 mins

Beef Hor Fun Wide Rice Noodles with Beef

This is a hearty and filling dish. Chris likes to mix the leftovers with a beaten egg and fry them slowly until crusty in a non-stick pan for breakfast.

250 g (9 oz) sirloin beef
2 tablespoons Shaoxing rice wine
1 1/2 tablespoons very finely grated
   ginger
1 teaspoon black pepper
2 tablespoons oyster sauce
2 tablespoons sesame oil
2 teaspoons cornflour
4 tablespoons vegetable oil
500 g (1 lb 2 oz) fresh *hor fun* (wide rice
   noodles)
2 tablespoons dark soy sauce
150 ml (2/3 cup minus 1 tablespoon) water
3 spring onions, sliced into 5-cm (2-in)
   lengths
pickled green chilies, to serve

1 Slice beef into thin strips. Mix with wine, ginger, pepper, oyster sauce, and sesame oil, then set aside to marinate, covered and refrigerated, for at least 20 minutes and up to 3 hours. When ready to cook, mix cornflour into beef.
2 Heat 3 tablespoons vegetable oil in a wok over high heat until smoking and quickly fry *hor fun* with dark soy sauce for 2 minutes, tossing vigorously, until slightly browned. Remove from wok.
3 Add remaining oil to wok and fry beef for 2 minutes. Add water and *hor fun* and fry 1 minute, then add spring onions and toss well 30 seconds more to wilt them. Serve immediately with pickled green chilies on the side.

Note *Hor fun* noodles are broader than *kway teow*. If you cannot find the former, use the widest *kway teow* you can find.

Serves 3–4
Cooking time: 6 mins
Preparation time: 15 mins plus 30 mins marinating time

Fishball and Glass Noodle Soup

The best fishballs can usually be found in good wet markets, but Asian grocery shops should also sell them vacuum-packed or loose.

875 ml (3$^1/_2$ cups) water
24 ready-made fishballs
1 fish or *ikan bilis* stock cube
$^1/_2$ tablespoon light soy sauce
2 tablespoons preserved salted vegetable
  (*tang chai*)
1 teaspoon white pepper
75 g (5$^1/_4$ oz) *tang hoon* (glass noodles or
  mung bean noodles), soaked in warm
  water until soft, about 5 minutes
2 spring onions, chopped, for garnish
sliced red chilies and light soy sauce,
  to serve

1 Bring water to the boil in a pot. Add fishballs and simmer gently for 3 minutes, then add stock cube, soy sauce, preserved cabbage, and pepper and simmer 3 minutes more.
2 Place 2 to 3 tablespoons of glass noodles into each serving bowl and top up with 4 fishballs and soup. Garnish with spring onions and serve with sliced red chilies and light soy sauce on the side.

Serves 6
Cooking time: 6 mins
Preparation time: 10 mins

Preserved vegetable for adding flavor.

Fried Hokkien Mee

Modern food-court versions of this are all too often terribly sloppy, in execution and texture. The old-fashioned version, after which this is patterned, was moist and highly fragrant and if taken away, was (and is still, occasionally) wrapped up in a large dried "opair" leaf, which added an ineffable kick to the aroma.

600 ml (2^1/$_3$ cups plus 1 tablespoon) water
450 g (1 lb) belly pork
4 tablespoons vegetable oil
2 tablespoons crushed garlic
300 g (10 oz) fresh yellow noodles
125 g (4^1/$_2$ oz) dried *bee hoon* (rice
   vermicelli), soaked in warm water
   10 minutes
250 g (9 oz) fresh prawns, shelled
1 piece fish cake, sliced
1 small squid, cleaned and head discarded,
   sliced into rings and tentacle clumps
75 g (2^3/$_4$ oz) Chinese chives, cut into
   5-cm (2-in) lengths
75 g (2^3/$_4$ oz) beansprouts
2 tablespoons fish sauce
^{3}/$_4$ teaspoon white pepper
^{1}/$_4$ teaspoon sugar
4 eggs
Sambal Blachan (p. 25) or Sambal Goreng
   (p. 28) sliced red chili, cut calamansi
   limes, to serve

Serves 3–4
Cooking time: 30 mins
Preparation time: 20 mins

1 Bring water to the boil in a large pot over medium heat. Add belly pork and simmer gently 20 minutes. Let pork sit in stock for 10 minutes, then remove and slice into bite-size strips. Measure out 250 ml (1 cup) stock and set aside.
2 Heat oil in a wok over very high heat. Fry crushed garlic for 30 seconds, until light browned and fragrant, then add both types of noodles and fry vigorously for 1 to 2 minutes or until noodles are very dry-looking but not burnt.
3 Add reserved stock — which the noodles should suck up rapidly — prawns, fish cake, squid, chives, beansprouts, fish sauce, pepper, and sugar and stir very vigorously for 3 to 4 minutes over high heat. Crack in eggs and stir well. They should set quickly. The noodles are done when they become moist but not soggy — add more stock if necessary — and seafood is fully cooked. Serve with accompaniments.

Bak Kut Teh   Pork Rib Soup

This robust soup is traditionally eaten as a breakfast dish with *yew char kway* (Chinese crullers) and a pot of Chinese tea on the side. *Bak kut teh* spice mixes are available in most Chinese grocery stores and supermarkets.

600 g (1 lb 5^1/$_2$ oz) pork ribs, cut into
  4-cm (2^3/$_4$-in) pieces
150 g (5^1/$_4$ oz) lean pork
1 cinnamon stick
5 cloves
1 sachet *bak kut teh* spices
2^1/$_2$ liters (10 cups) water or pork stock
3 tablespoons light soy sauce
1 teaspoon salt
1 teaspoon sugar
***yew char kway* (Chinese crullers) and**
  chopped fresh coriander leaves,
  to serve

Serves 3–4
Cooking time: 1 hour 15 mins
Preparation time: 10 mins

1 Combine pork ribs, lean pork, cinnamon, cloves, *bak kut teh* sachets, and water in a large pot. Bring to a boil over medium heat, adjust heat to low and simmer, covered, for 30 minutes.
2 Add soy sauce, salt, and sugar and simmer for 45 minutes more, or until pork is fork tender.
3 Remove lean pork and shred into small pieces. Strain stock into serving bowls and divide lean pork and pork ribs between them. Serve with *yew char kway* and chopped fresh coriander.

Note Every hawker stall puts a different spin on this dish. Some season it with dark soy sauce, others with light: use what you prefer. *Bak kut teh* spice sachets can be bought at Chinese grocery stores or herbal medical halls.

Different versions of noodles in spicy broths, sometimes containing coconut, sometimes not, can be found across the length and breadth of the Malay peninsula. Penang, Malacca, Kuala Lumpur, and Johor *laksa* are all different. Sarawak has its own version, and so does Singapore. The admittedly unorthodox cut lime is in the photo because Chris likes to squeeze it over the *sambal*, to cut the richness of the gravy.

4 tablespoons dried shrimps, soaked
  until soft
6 tablespoons vegetable oil
1 teaspoon salt
2 teaspoons sugar
1¹/₂ liters (6 cups) thin coconut milk
600 g (1 lb 5¹/₂ oz) fresh *laksa* noodles
  (or cooked somen)
100 g (3¹/₂ oz) beansprouts
16 large prawns
150 g (5¹/₄ oz) blood cockles (optional)
large handful finely shredded *laksa* leaves
  (*daun kesom*) and Sambal Goreng
  (p. 28), to serve

Spice Paste
300 g (10¹/₂ oz) onions, sliced
6 cloves garlic
12 dried chilies, soaked until soft
3 stalks lemongrass
5 slices galangal
1 tablespoon shrimp paste
1 thumb-sized piece fresh turmeric,
  peeled

Serves 4–6
Cooking time: 16 mins
Preparation time: 20 mins

1 Grind Spice Paste ingredients until fine. Grind dried shrimps until fine and set aside.

2 Heat oil in a wok over medium heat and fry Spice Paste for 6 to 8 minutes, until thickened and fragrant. Add coconut milk, bring to a boil and add salt, sugar, and dried shrimps. Simmer uncovered for 5 minutes and adjust taste with salt or sugar as necessary.

3 Blanch noodles and beansprouts separately in boiling water for 30 seconds. Blanch prawns in fresh boiling water for 2 minutes or until cooked through, then drain, shell and slice in half lengthwise. Blanch cockles, if using, in boiling water for 1 minute. Discard unopened cockles and remove cooked ones from their shells.

4 To serve, divide beansprouts and noodles between serving bowls and garnish with sliced prawns and cockles. Ladle gravy over and let diners help themselves to *laksa* leaves and *sambal*.

Note "Katong style" *laksa*, a "brand name" claimed by several different and competing Singaporean stalls over the last few years, is distinguished by thick, coconut-heavy gravy and soft noodles cut into short lengths, to be eaten with a spoon only and no chopsticks. Frankly, we will always prefer homemade.

Fresh blood cockles at a wet market.

Sayur Lodeh   Mixed Vegetables in Coconut Milk

A very simple, very tasty vegetable stew mandatory at every *nasi padang* (Malay rice and cooked dishes) stall. Serve it with compressed rice slices (*lemang*) and *serondeng* for a complete meal.

1 brinjal
12 French beans, topped and tailed
2 small carrots
200 g (7 oz) cabbage
5 tablespoons vegetable oil
500 ml (2 cups) coconut milk
190 ml (3/4 cup) water
1 teaspoon salt
1 teaspoon sugar

Spice Paste
6 candlenuts
10 shallots
2 teaspoons shrimp paste
1 teaspoon dried shrimp, soaked
  until soft
1 thumb-sized piece fresh turmeric
3 cloves garlic
4–6 red chilies

1 Halve brinjal lengthwise and slice across into half moons about 1 cm ($^1/_2$ in) thick. Slice the french beans diagonally in half, the carrots into 4-cm ($1^3/_4$-in) sticks, and the cabbage into wide strips. Grind all Spice Paste ingredients fine.

2 Heat oil in a wok over medium heat and fry ground spices until fragrant, 4 to 5 minutes. Add coconut milk and water and bring to the boil. Add all vegetables and simmer for 10 minutes.

3 Add salt and sugar and simmer for 5 minutes more or until vegetables are tender. Serve hot.

Serves 3–4
Cooking time: 20 mins
Preparation time: 10 mins

Rojak   Fragrant Spicy Salad

Is it Chinese? Is it Malay? Whichever, this is a true son of the Singapore soil, once sold only by street hawkers. A spicy salad bar none and a production number that should be stirred up in front of your adoring guests! Don't let it sit around, as it waters out after a while.

120 g (4$^1/_2$ oz) beansprouts, washed and drained
150 g (5$^1/_4$ oz) kangkong (water con- volvulus)
4 fried beancurd squares (*tau pok*)
2 *yew char kway* (Chinese crullers)
200 g (7 oz) *bangkwang* (yambean or jicama), peeled
150 g (5$^1/_4$ oz) fresh pineapple
1 cucumber
1 small ginger bud (*bunga kantan*), shredded

Dressing
1 tablespoon tamarind pulp
150 ml ($^2/_3$ cup minus 1 tablespoon) water
1 generous tablespoon shrimp paste
4 red chilies, finely chopped
1 tablespoon sugar
3 tablespoons *hae koh* (shrimp sauce)
3 calamansi limes
4 tablespoons coarsely ground peanuts

1 Trim off and discard 2$^1/_2$ cm (1 in) from the root ends of the kangkong, and wash well. Bring a large pot of water to a rolling boil. Blanch beansprouts for 30 seconds, then remove and drain. Blanch kangkong for 1 minute or until just tender, and drain. Chop kangkong into 5-cm (2-in) lengths. Toast crullers and beancurd under a hot grill until they are crisp on the outside, 4 to 5 minutes, turning frequently.
2 To make Dressing, knead tamarind with water until pulp dissolves, then strain. Toast shrimp paste over a live flame until crusty and fragrant (see Sambal Blachan recipe, p. 25). Grind chilies, shrimp paste, and sugar until fine, and transfer to a large mixing bowl.
3 Stir shrimp paste into chili mixture until smooth. Slowly stir in lime juice and $^2/_3$ of the tamarind liquid. Taste it: it should be hot, sweet, sharp, and smoky. Add more sugar, tamarind liquid, or lime juice as necessary.
4 Add beansprouts and water convolvulus to bowl. With a sharp knife, slice in pineapple, *bangkwang*, cucumber, beancurd in bite-sized chunks. Toss well. Snip in fried beancurd and crullers with sharp scissors. Sprinkle in most of the ground peanuts and toss again. Serve sprinkled with more ground peanuts and shredded ginger bud.

Serves 4–5
Cooking time: 7 mins
Preparation time: 20 mins

Squeeze lime juice into the sauce mixture.

"Shave" the cucumber into the mixing bowl.

Sprinkle in the peanuts and mix well.

Chili Crab

One of our unofficial national dishes, once served up by stalls on the banks of the Kallang River, up north in Punggol, and — still — on the East Coast. Chili crab today has several different incarnations. The gravy may be sweet, tart, and ketchuppy, or slicked with chili oil, or thickened with beaten eggs, or grainy with onions and chopped peanuts, or even made tangy with orange juice. One thing is constant: the crabs (usually Sri Lankan green crabs) must be meaty and impeccably fresh.

3 large fresh crabs
5 tablespoons vegetable oil
1 large onion, sliced
8 cloves garlic, finely minced
2 tablespoons grated ginger
5–6 tablespoons hot chili sauce, such as
  Thai *sriracha* sauce
4 tablespoons tomato ketchup
1 teaspoon salt
1 teaspoon sugar
375 ml (1 1/2 cups) water
baguette slices, to serve

Serves 2–4
Cooking time: 10 mins
Preparation time: 20 mins

1 Remove body shell of crabs and discard lungs and fibrous tissue. Cut main body into half down the center line, then cut each half into two pieces. Separate claws from body and crack them lightly.

2 Heat oil in a wok over high heat and fry sliced onions vigorously until softened, about 3 minutes. Add garlic and ginger and fry 1 to 2 minutes more or until fragrant. Add crabs and fry vigorously for 5 minutes until they turn bright red.

3 Add all remaining ingredients and stir for 1 to 3 minutes more or until gravy has thickened to coat the crab pieces. Serve with chunks of baguette to mop up the gravy.

Note The character of this simple version of chili crab changes with the kind of chili sauce you use. We prefer a pulpy one like *sriracha*, as opposed to a sugary, syrupy one like Lingham's. You can even use Sambal Goreng (p. 28), which makes the gravy more drily pungent.

If you are squeamish about preparing live crabs, blanch them in boiling water for 6 minutes before chopping them up, then fry for 2 minutes only in Step 2.

Crabs, with rich orange roe, at a market.

Hainanese Pork Chops

One can believe this dish held sway in British colonial homes and country clubs, whose cooks were drawn from the Hainanese community. The necessary presence of HP sauce in the gravy is a clue.

4 thick boneless pork chops
25 cream crackers
2 large eggs, well beaten
Oil for deep-frying
2 potatoes, peeled and sliced 1-cm
  ($^1/_2$-in) thick
1 large onion, sliced
1 tablespoon HP sauce
2 teaspoons light soy sauce
$1^1/_2$ tablespoons ketchup
$^1/_4$ teaspoon salt
2 teaspoons sugar
2 teaspoons cornflour
160 ml ($^2/_3$ cup) water
2 tomatoes, quartered
150 g (5 oz) frozen peas

Serves 3–4
Cooking time: 15 mins
Preparation time: 20 mins

1 Sandwich the chops between two sheets of plastic wrap and beat lightly with a meat mallet or blunt cleaver spine to flatten them to a 1-cm ($^1/_2$-in) thickness.
2 Crush cream crackers into fine crumbs. Turn chops in egg to coat, then in cracker crumbs, patting them on in a even layer and shaking off excess. Repeat egging and crumbing to get a secure, even coating.
3 Heat oil in a wok until shimmering and giving off haze, then deep-fry pork chops two at a time until golden brown, turning once, about 4 to 6 minutes per batch. Remove and drain well on kitchen paper.
4 Remove all but 3 tablespoons of oil from wok and fry potatoes over medium heat for 5 minutes, turning frequently, until browned and tender. Remove and drain. Fry onions in remaining oil until soft, 2 to 3 minutes, then add all remaining ingredients except tomatoes and peas. Bring to the boil, add tomatoes, peas, and potatoes and simmer for 1 minute, until thickened. Slice pork chops and pour gravy over to serve.

Note Crushed crackers are more authentic, but for a crispier finish, use *panko* (Japanese breadcrumbs).

Pork Satay

A Chinese spin on a dish also popularized by Malay hawker stalls, who use beef, mutton, and chicken for their satays, and serve the sauce sans pineapple. Some culinary scholars trace the word "*satay*" to the Hokkien "*sar tei*" which means three pieces, a reference to the morsels of meat on the stick.

750 g (1 lb 11 oz) pork rib-eye steaks
2 stalks lemongrass, bruised at root end
** to make basting brushes**
oil, for basting chunkily diced cucumber
red onions and *ketupat* (pressed rice cake),
** to serve**

Marinade
2 tablespoons ground coriander
1 tablespoon ground cumin
1 teaspoon ground fennel
1 teaspoon ground turmeric
6 shallots, minced
2 stalks lemongrass, thinly sliced
3 cloves garlic, minced
1 teaspoon salt
1 tablespoon sugar
3 tablespoons vegetable oil

1 Soak 30 to 40 long bamboo skewers in cold water for at least 2 hours, to prevent them from burning later.
2 Cut pork into small strips about 2$^1/_2$ cm (1 in) long and 1 cm ($^1/_2$ in) thick. Grind Marinade ingredients to a very fine paste and mix with pork. Let marinate, covered and refrigerated, at least 5 hours or overnight.
3 Thread 4 to 5 pieces on pointed end of each skewer, pressing them together. Grill skewers over charcoal or under a very hot grill, using lemongrass brush to baste with oil occasionally, for 5 to 6 minutes, turning once or twice. Serve hot with sauce, onions, cucumber, and *ketupat*.

Serves 4–6
Cooking time: 5–6 minutes per batch of satay
Preparation time: 20 mins + 5 hours marinating

Satay Sauce

2$^1/_2$ tablespoons tamarind pulp
625 ml (2$^1/_2$ cups) water
6 tablespoons vegetable oil
2 tablespoons sugar, or to taste
400 g (14$^1/_4$ oz) roasted unsalted
** peanuts**
400 g (14$^1/_4$ oz) canned crushed
** pineapple**

Spice Paste
8 dried chilies, soaked till soft
20 shallots
3 cloves garlic
1 tablespoon shrimp paste
8 candlenuts
2 stalks lemongrass
4 thin slices galangal

1 Grind all Spice Paste ingredients until fine. Knead tamarind with water until pulp dissolves and strain. Whizz peanuts in food processor until very finely chopped.
2 Heat oil in a wok over medium heat and fry Spice Paste 5 minutes, until thickened and fragrant. Add tamarind liquid and simmer for 10 minutes, then add sugar and peanuts. Taste and adjust seasoning. Pour into serving bowls — one for each person — and add a dollop of crushed pineapple to each bowl. Serve sauce and any extra pineapple on the side, with *satay*.

Serves 4–6
Cooking time: 15 minutes
Preparation time: 15 minutes

Soup Kambing   Spiced Mutton Soup

A fragrant mutton soup, always served with crusty baguette on the side. Lamb, which makes a milder-flavored soup, can be used instead of mutton, but reduce the cooking time slightly.

7 tablespoons oil
10 shallots, sliced
400 g (14^1/$_4$ oz) mutton, cut into shreds
1^1/$_2$ liters (6 cups) lamb or chicken stock
    or water
1 cinnamon stick
^{1}/$_2$ star anise
4 cardamom pods
1 teaspoon salt
1 teaspoon freshly ground black pepper
large handful fresh coriander leaves, for
    garnish
baguette slices, to serve

Spice Paste
5 shallots
4 cloves garlic
4 slices fresh ginger
1 teaspoon grated fresh turmeric
1 teaspoon ground cumin
1 teaspoon ground fennel
2 tablespoons ground coriander

1 Heat oil in a wok over medium-low heat. Fry sliced shallots, stirring, until crisp and golden brown, 4 to 6 minutes. Drain on kitchen paper and set aside. (You can save the oil for use as a condiment.)
2 Grind Spice Paste ingredients until very fine and mix with mutton. Let marinate at room temperature, covered, for 1 hour.
3 Bring stock to the boil in a large pot. Add cinnamon, star anise, cardamoms, mutton with all its marinade, salt, and pepper. Let it bubble vigorously for 15 minutes, then cover pot, reduce heat and simmer gently for 40 minutes, covered. Serve garnished with coriander leaves and chunks of French baguette.

Serves 3–4
Cooking time: 1 hour
Preparation time: 15 mins + 1 hour marinating time

See Yow Kai Soy-braised Chicken

Cantonese in origin. Leftover sauce can be used to braise another chicken, or in fact any meat.

3 tablespoons vegetable oil
3 tablespoons sugar
1 whole chicken, about 1^1/$_2$ kg (3^1/$_4$ lbs),
   excess fat removed
1^1/$_2$ liters (6 cups) water
5 tablespoons thick dark soy sauce
large walnut-sized knob galangal, bruised
^{3}/$_4$ teaspoon five-spice powder
1 teaspoon salt
sliced cucumber and slivered spring
   onions, to serve
3 tablespoons sesame oil

Serves 4–5
Cooking time: 1 hour
Preparation time: 10 mins

1 Heat oil and sugar together in a wok over medium heat, stirring frequently. Watch it like a hawk; when sugar has melted and caramelized into little brown globules, add chicken and roll over several times to coat.
2 Add water, soy sauce, galangal, five-spice powder, and salt and bring to a boil. Reduce heat to low and simmer gently, covered, for 45 to 50 minutes, turning chicken once, or until chicken is tender but not falling apart. Let chicken sit in hot liquid, covered, for 10 minutes.
3 Gently lift out chicken and transfer to chopping board. Carve into small pieces. Pull stray bits of meat off bones and heap into a mound on a serving platter, then surround with pieces. Garnish plate with cucumber and spring onions.
4 Add sesame oil to sauce and reduce over high heat until slightly thickened, 6 to 8 minutes. Drizzle a little sauce over chicken and serve extra on the side.

Note You can also braise a duck in the same way; use 2 ^{1}/$_2$ liters (10 cups) water and simmer duck for 2 hours.

Ikan Panggang Barbecued Fish

Just about any firm-fleshed fish can be cooked this way, preferably on the bone for more flavor and the better for the fish to hold its shape.

2 whole fish, about 450 g (1 lb)
pinch salt

Sauce
1 tablespoon shrimp paste
4 red chilies
2 cloves garlic
3 tablespoons *ketjap manis* or thick dark
   sweet soy sauce
2 tablespoons lime juice

Serves 4–5
Cooking time: 16 mins
Preparation time: 10 mins

1 Toast shrimp paste over a live flame until crusty (see Sambal Blachan recipe on p. 25). Grind with chilies and garlic until fine, then mix with *ketjap manis* and lime juice.
2 Pre-heat grill. Make one or two deep slashes across thickest part of fish, and sprinkle lightly with salt. Place in a grill pan lined with oiled foil or washed banana leaves. Grill for about 8 minutes on each side, turning once, or until meat comes away from the bone easily.
3 Spread Sauce over grilled fish and serve immediately. Alternatively, serve Sauce on the side.

Homestyle Dishes

Some local dishes lack the grandeur required for a banquet, the finesse demanded by a gourmet spread, or the pomp and circumstance of festive fare: but they have flavour, humility and sheer *oomph* to spare. These belong on that beloved and most iconic Asian dining arena: the home table.

To be sure, everything in this book can be cooked at home, but these are some of the dishes that are dished out from the wok most often when we're feeling cerebrally-challenged at the end of a long day.

Shrimp Fried Rice

This is basic recipe that you can embellish at will, with vegetables, herbs, and the like.

1 tablespoon oil
3 cloves garlic, minced
2 eggs
150 g (5^1/$_4$ oz) fresh shrimps, shelled
250 g (9 oz) cold, cooked rice
1 tablespoon light soy sauce
^{1}/$_2$ teaspoon black pepper
^{1}/$_2$ teaspoon salt
pickled green chilies, to serve

1 Heat oil in a wok over high heat and fry garlic 1 minute, until lightly browned. Crack in eggs and stir for a few seconds until they are almost set, then chop them roughly with the edge of the wok ladle.
2 Add shrimps and toss for 2 minutes, then add all remaining ingredients and fry about 3 minutes more until rice is heated through and the shrimps are fully cooked. Serve hot with pickled green chilies on the side.

Serves 2
Cooking time: 7 mins
Preparation time: 5 mins

One-Pot Rice and Chicken with Oyster Sauce

The microwave makes this dish super-easy to whip up.

200 g (7 oz) rice
350 ml (1^1/$_3$ cups plus 1 tablespoon)
  water
200 g (7 oz) skinless boneless chicken
  thigh or breast
2 tablespoons oyster sauce
1 tablespoon dark soy sauce
^{1}/$_2$ teaspoon sugar
1 teaspoon white or black pepper
4 slices ginger
chopped spring onions and sliced red chili,
  to serve

1 Wash rice well and combine with water in a microwave-safe bowl with a cover. Cover and microwave for 8 minutes on high.
2 While rice cooks, cut chicken into cubes and mix with oyster sauce, soy sauce, sugar, pepper, and ginger.
3 Stir chicken mixture into rice, cover, and microwave for 9 to 10 minutes more. Let rice stand 3 minutes before serving, sprinkled with chopped spring onions.

Serves 2
Cooking time: 20 mins
Preparation time: 10 mins

Lohan Chai   Buddha's Vegetarian Feast

A slightly simplified version; the original contains 18 ingredients that symbolize Buddha's 18 disciples. This rich and filling vegetarian dish is especially cheered at reunion dinner on the eve of Chinese New Year, and is appreciated for its flavor by any Chinese household, whatever their religion.

20 mange-tout, topped and tailed
20 French beans, sliced
1 large carrot, sliced thinly
12 Chinese mushrooms, soaked in hot
    water 1 hour and halved
1 can straw mushrooms, drained
1 can gingko nuts, drained
1 can lotus seeds, drained
200 g (7 oz) bok choy (Chinese cabbage),
    cut into broad strips
4 pieces sweet beancurd wafers (*tim
    choke*), rinse in warm water and cut
    into thin strips
small handful of black moss fungus
    (*fatt choi*)
4 tablespoons vegetable oil
3 cloves garlic, crushed
5 slices ginger
3 cubes fermented red beancurd (*lam yee*)
2 tablespoons hoi sin sauce
2 tablespoons light soy sauce
1 liter (4 cups) water

1 Wash and cut up all vegetables. Rinse and thoroughly drain straw mushrooms, gingko nuts, and lotus seeds. Rinse beancurd wafers in warm water and snip into 1-cm (1/2-in) wide strips with scissors. Soak black moss fungus in tepid water for 5 minutes, then drain well.
2 Heat oil in a wok over high heat and fry garlic and ginger for 1 to 2 minutes, until fragrant. Reduce heat to low and add fermented beancurd. Mash lightly with wok ladle and add hoi sin sauce, soy sauce, and all vegetables. Stir well and add water. Bring to a boil and simmer for 25 to 30 minutes or until gravy is rich and thick and vegetables are tender. Serve hot.

Note This can keep for several days refrigerated. Reheat fully to serve.

Serves 4–6
Cooking time: 35 mins
Preparation time: 20 mins

Red fermented beancurd has a sweet richness.

Stir-fried Beansprouts, Chives, and Beancurd

150 g (5¹/₄ oz) beansprouts
100 g (3¹/₂ oz) Chinese chives (*koo chai*)
150 g (5¹/₄ oz) firm beancurd (*tau kwa*)
1 tablespoon oil
2 garlic cloves, minced
³/₄ teaspoon salt

Serves 2–3
Cooking time: 6 mins
Preparation time: 10 mins

1 Rinse and pat dry beansprouts. Nip off roots and remove any brown seed caps. Cut chives into 5-cm (2-in) lengths, wash, and pat dry. Dice beancurd.
2 Heat oil in a wok over high heat and fry garlic for 1 minute or until lightly browned. Add beancurd and fry, stirring gently, for 2 to 3 minutes, until browned all over. Add all other ingredients and fry vigorously for 2 minutes until vegetables are cooked. Serve immediately.

Spicy Long Beans

A standard item seen on Chinese and Malay cooked-food hawker stalls. Any kind of long bean and even asparagus can be cooked this way.

15 long beans
4 tablespoons oil
1 tablespoon fish sauce
1 teaspoon sugar
100 ml (¹/₃ cup plus 1 tablespoon) water

Spice Paste
1 stalk lemongrass
3 slices galangal
3 red chilies
5 candlenuts
1 tablespoon shrimp paste
10 shallots
5 cloves garlic

1 Cut long beans into 5-cm (2-in) lengths, wash, and drain. Grind Spice Paste ingredients until fine.

2 Heat oil in a wok over medium heat and fry Spice Paste until thickened and fragrant, 5 to 7 minutes. Add long beans, fish sauce, and sugar and stir-fry for 5 to 7 minutes, until beans are tender. Sprinkle water over as you fry — you may not need all of it. When done the beans should be moist but not swimming in liquid. Serve with hot rice.

Serves 3–4
Cooking time: 15 mins
Preparation time: 10 mins

Kangkong Blachan   Water Convolvulus with Shrimp Paste Sambal

A simple preparation with wonderfully punchy flavor. Any green vegetable with a succulent texture benefits from this treatment.

250 g (9 oz) kangkong (water convolvulus)
1 tablespoon shrimp paste
2 tablespoons dried shrimps, soaked
  until soft
4 red chilies
4 cloves garlic
4 tablespoons oil
150 ml ($^2/_3$ cup minus 1 tablespoon) water

Serves 3–4
Cooking time: 8 mins
Preparation time: 15 mins

1 Cut off and discard $2^1/_2$ cm (1 in) from kangkong root ends. Slice stalks into $7^1/_2$ cm (3 in) lengths, then rinse very well in a basin of cold water to remove grit.
2 Grind shrimp paste with dried shrimps, chilies, and garlic until fine. Heat oil in a wok over medium-high heat and fry paste vigorously for 3 to 4 minutes until fragrant.
3 Add kangkong and stir-fry for 2 minutes, then add water and stir 1 minute more. Serve immediately.

Spicy Okra with Prawns

Okra or ladies' fingers, also known as *bindi* or *kacang lindeh*, are a versatile vegetable by virtue of their succulent plainness. They make fine addition to many curries, and are wonderful just simply steamed whole and eaten with spicy sambal and lime juice.

16 okra
3 tablespoons oil
300 g (10 1/2 oz) peeled fresh prawns
1 teaspoon salt
2 tablespoons lime juice
5 tablespoons water
1 teaspoon sugar

Spice Paste
3 red chilies
10 shallots
2 stalks lemongrass
6 candlenuts
1 scant teaspoon shrimp paste
3/4 teaspoon ground turmeric

1 Trim off okra stems and pointed tips. Cut okra into bite-sized lengths and blanch in boiling water for 1 1/2 minutes, then drain well and rinse with cold water. This helps to reduce its stickiness.
2 Grind Spice Paste ingredients until fine. Heat oil in a wok over medium-high heat and fry paste until thickened and fragrant, 3 to 4 minutes.
3 Add okra and stir-fry for 1 minute, then add all remaining ingredients and fry for 3 to 4 minutes until prawns are cooked through. Serve immediately.

Serves 3–4
Cooking time: 10 mins
Preparation time: 15 mins

Foo Yong Hai   Scrambled Eggs with Prawns, Carrot, and Marrow

Otherwise known (and frequently corrupted) as egg foo yong. If you're in the mood for luxury, substitute crabmeat or scallops for the prawns.

1 large carrot
1 ridged loofah (*chi kwa*)
5 eggs
4 tablespoons milk
1 tablespoon light soy sauce
$^1/_2$ teaspoon white pepper
$^1/_2$ teaspoon salt
4 tablespoons oil
2 cloves garlic, crushed
200 g (7 oz) raw shrimps, peeled

Serves 2–3
Cooking time: 7 mins
Preparation time: 10 mins

1 Peel and slice carrots into 5 cm (2 in) long matchsticks. Peel loofah and remove soft core, then slice into batons.
2 Beat eggs with milk, soy sauce, pepper, and salt. Heat oil in a wok over medium heat and fry garlic for 1 minute, until light brown. Add carrots and marrow and stir-fry for 3 minutes.
3 Add shrimps and stir-fry for $1^1/_2$ minutes. Slowly pour in egg mixture, stirring gently to scramble. When eggs are softly set, dish up and serve immediately.

Note The addition of a little milk makes the egg mixture softer and smoother.

Stir-Fried Beef with Kai Lan

A simple but delicious combination. This dish waits for no man, cook it quick, and eat it promptly while the *wok hei* — the "breath of the wok" — still wafts about the plate.

350 g (12¹/₂ oz) kai lan (Chinese kale)
200 g (7 oz) beef sirloin
2 teaspoons cornstarch
2 teaspoons light soy sauce
3 tablespoons Shaoxing wine
2 tablespoons vegetable oil
3 cloves garlic, crushed
1 tablespoon finely chopped ginger
2 tablespoons oyster sauce
1 tablespoon sesame oil
1 teaspoon black pepper
4 tablespoons water

1 Cut kai lan into 5 cm (2 in) lengths, wash and drain well. Slice beef into thin strips and mix with cornstarch, light soy sauce, and half the Shaoxing wine.
2 Heat oil in a wok over high heat. Fry garlic and ginger until golden brown, about 1 minute, then add beef slices and stir-fry vigorously for 1 minute. Add kai lan and fry for 2 minutes.
3 Add remaining wine and all other ingredients and stir-fry for 1 to 2 minutes more, or until juices are thickened and kai lan is crisp-tender. Serve immediately.

Serves 2–3
Cooking time: 6 minutes
Preparation time: 15 mins

Pumpkin Braised with Dried Shrimp

An old-fashioned Chinese recipe. Japanese Kabocha squash and Australian blue-skinned pumpkin work very well with this recipe — in fact often better than our local brown pumpkins, which can be watery.

1 small pumpkin, about 20 to 25 cm
  (about 8–10 in) across
1 tablespoon oil
4 cloves garlic, minced
1$^1/_2$ tablespoons dried shrimp, soaked
  till soft
2 tablespoons Shaoxing wine
190 ml ($^3/_4$ cup) chicken or pork stock or
  water
2 teaspoons light soy sauce
$^3/_4$ teaspoon salt

1 Slice pumpkin into wedges about 3 cm (1$^1/_2$ in) thick. (Using a heavy cleaver is easiest.) Cut off and discard skin, seeds, and fibers, then cut each wedge across into 3 pieces.
2 Heat oil in a wok over medium heat. Add garlic and fry 1 minute, then add dried shrimp and fry 1 minute more. Add wine, stock, soy sauce, salt, and pumpkin. Bring to a boil, then partially cover and reduce heat to medium-low. Simmer, stirring frequently, until pumpkin is tender and gravy is reduced to a couple of spoonfuls, 10 to 15 minutes.

Serves 3–4
Cooking time: 17 mins
Preparation time: 15 mins

Braised Chicken Wings with Dried Beancurd and Water Convolvulus

Not often seen outside the home nowadays but a very traditional recipe, this is also known as *lo kai yik*. Serve it with hot rice and a red chili, garlic, and vinegar dip.

150 g (5¼ oz) kangkong (water
  convolvulus)
2 firm beancurd squares (*tau kwa*)
3 tablespoons oil
1½ tablespoons chopped garlic
1½ tablespoons chopped ginger
2 cubes fermented red beancurd
  (*lam yee*)
1 tablespoon hoi sin sauce
2 tablespoons oyster sauce
12 chicken wings, each cut into 3 joints
750 ml (3 cups) water

1 Trim off root ends of kangkong. Blanch kangkong in boiling water for 2 minutes, then drain well. Tie pairs of stalks into loose knots. Cut each beancurd square into 8 triangles.
2 Heat oil in a wok over medium heat and fry garlic and ginger for 2 minutes. Add fermented beancurd and mash well with wok ladle, then stir in hoi sin sauce, oyster sauce, chicken wings, and water and simmer uncovered for 20 minutes.
3 Add kangkong and beancurd and simmer for 5 minutes more. Dish up and serve immediately.

Serves 4–6
Cooking time: 30 mins
Preparation time: 15 mins

Soto Ayam   Spiced Chicken Soup

One of our ultimate cold-weather favorites.

4 tablespoons vegetable oil
1¼ liters (5 cups) water or chicken stock
1 whole chicken, cleaned
1 teaspoon salt
2 potatoes, boiled, peeled, and diced
90 g (3 oz) *tang hoon* (mung bean
   vermicelli), soaked in lukewarm water
   10 minutes
fresh coriander or Chinese celery leaves,
   for garnish

Spices
6 candlenuts
1 teaspoon black peppercorns
10 shallots
5 cloves garlic
1 thumb-sized piece fresh turmeric
4 slices ginger
2 stalks lemongrass

Sauce
6 chili padi, pounded to a coarse paste
2 tablespoons dark soy sauce
2 tablespoons lime juice
1 teaspoon sugar

1 To prepare the Spices, grind candlenuts and peppercorns together to a coarse powder. Chop remaining spices very fine. Heat oil in a wok over medium heat and fry all spices together for 4 minutes, until fragrant. Add water, chicken, and salt and simmer, partially covered, for 35 minutes.
2 Let chicken sit in hot stock for 10 minutes, then transfer to chopping board. Discard skin. Pull meat off bones and shred into bite-sized pieces. Return bones to stock and simmer, covered, 10 minutes.
3 Divide vermicelli, chicken meat, and diced potatoes between serving bowls. Strain stock and ladle into bowls, then sprinkle with coriander leaves. Combine Sauce ingredients and serve on the side.

Note To turn this soup into a complete meal, add handful each of blanched fresh yellow noodles and beansprouts to each bowl. Or you could eat it with *ketupat* (compressed rice).

Serves 4–6
Cooking time: 50 minutes
Preparation time: 25 minutes + 10 minutes standing time

Ayam Tempra Spicy-sour Stir-fried Chicken

A recipe of hazy Portuguese ancestry, given a spicy fillip with aromatics like lemon grass, garlic, and lime leaves, for a hot, sweet, and sour flavor that is unique. This is Chris's current take on a dish that has been in the family for decades.

4 large chicken thighs or breasts, deboned
1/2 teaspoon shrimp paste
1 tablespoon palm sugar, finely chopped
1 tablespoon water
2 tablespoons *ketjap manis* (thick dark soy sauce), or dark soy sauce
2 tablespoons oil
1 onion, halved and sliced thickly
2 red chilies, sliced diagonally
3 cloves garlic, sliced
1 stalk lemongrass, sliced thinly on the diagonal
3 tablespoons freshly-squeezed lime juice
1/3 teaspoon salt, or to taste

1 Cut chicken into large bite-sized chunks. Mash shrimp paste with palm sugar, water, and *ketjap manis* until smooth, and mix with the chicken. Let marinate 15 minutes at room temperature.

2 Heat oil in a wok over high heat. Add onion, chilies, garlic, and lemongrass and stir-fry vigorously until softened and fragrant, 1 to 2 minutes. Add chicken and fry until it is just cooked through, 3 to 4 minutes more, then add lime juice and salt and mix well. Serve hot with rice.

Serves 2–3
Cooking time: 6 mins
Preparation time: 10 mins + 15 mins marinating time

Chicken Wings and Mushrooms in Chinese Wine

This dish is hearty and robust, very fragrant, and easily multiplied if you're cooking for a crowd.

8 chicken wings, each cut into 3 joints
80 ml (¹/₃ cup) Shaoxing wine
2 tablespoons sesame oil
1 teaspoon black pepper
8 Chinese dried mushrooms, soaked till
    soft and hard stalks removed
1 teaspoon salt
1 teaspoon sugar
2 tablespoons dark soy sauce
6 slices of fresh ginger
2 stalks spring onions, cut into 3-cm
    (1¹/₂-in) lengths
1 tablespoon chopped celery leaves
450 ml (2 cups) water

1 Combine wings with wine, sesame oil, and black pepper and let marinate for 1 hour, covered, at cool room temperature.
2 Halve mushrooms. Combine wings, mushrooms, and all other ingredients except spring onions and celery leaves in a large pot. Bring to the boil over medium heat, partially cover and simmer for 20 minutes, or until wings are tender. Increase heat to reduce sauce more during the last 5 minutes, if desired. Stir in spring onions and celery leaves and cook 1 minute more, then dish up. Serve piping hot.

Serves 3–4
Cooking time: 25 mins
Preparation time: 10 mins

Lemon Chicken

One of those dishes that can be horrifying in the wrong hands (glutinous sauce, greasy chicken) but which has real elegance in its rightful Cantonese purity. The sauce also goes brilliantly with battered strips of white fish.

2 chicken breasts, skinned and deboned
1 egg, lightly beaten
4 tablespoons cornflour
oil for deep-frying
grated lemon zest for garnish, if desired

Sauce
3 tablespoons lemon juice
2 tablespoons plum sauce
200 ml ($^3/_4$ cup) water
2 teaspoons cornflour
$^1/_2$ lemon, scrubbed, quartered, and sliced paper thin

1 Stir all Sauce ingredients together and set aside.
2 Lightly beat chicken breasts to a thickness of $1^1/_2$ cm ($^2/_3$ in). Coat chicken with beaten egg and dredge with cornflour. Heat oil in a wok over medium heat until shimmering, and deep-fry chicken until light golden brown, 5 to 7 minutes, turning once. Drain on kitchen paper and set aside.
3 Transfer Sauce mixture to a small non-reactive pot and bring to a boil over medium heat. Simmer 2 minutes or until it thickens. Slice chicken into serving pieces, pour sauce over and serve immediately, garnished with lemon zest if desired.

Serves 2–3
Cooking time: 10 mins
Preparation time: 15 mins

Deep-fried Pepper Squid

Not crunchy as a fritter would be, but tender and toothsome.

2 large squid
1 tablespoon coarsely ground black
   pepper
1 teaspoon caster (superfine) sugar
1 tablespoon cornflour
Oil for deep-frying
1 teaspoon sea salt
cut limes, to serve

Serves 2–3
Cooking time: 5 mins
Preparation time: 10 mins

1 Wash squid. Pull out, cut off, and discard head. Cut tentacles into small clumps. Slit body tube and open out flat. Pull off skin. Score parallel lines lengthwise along inside of body tube, then slice across into thin strips. Dry squid well with paper towels. Mix squid with pepper, sugar, and cornflour.
2 Heat oil in a wok over high heat until shimmering and giving off a light haze, about 190°C (375°F). Slip squid into oil, separating the pieces with chopsticks. Fry in small batches, for 45 seconds per batch until squid pieces curl up and brown very lightly. Sprinkle with salt and serve with limes on the side.

Note If you can get hold of baby squid, which are about 4 cm (1$^1/_2$ in) long, use them instead, but deep-fry them until browned and crisp. Serve with sweet flour sauce as a dip.

Grilled Mackerel with Coriander

Mackerel is probably one of the most underrated fish around, maybe because it is inexpensive and therefore, sniffed at, maybe because it doesn't stay fresh for long. Its natural oils, high in omega-3 fatty acids, make it a prime candidate for grilling.

3 whole mackerel
2 teaspoons sea salt
2 teaspoons black pepper
2 tablespoons sunflower oil
3 tablespoons finely chopped fresh
** coriander**
cut limes, to serve

Serves 5–6
Cooking time: 20 mins
Preparation time: 10 mins

1 Pat each fish dry and make a few deep slashes through thickest part of body. Rub all over with salt, pepper, and oil. Place fish on a grill rack or roasting pan lined with greased foil, and cook under a very hot grill for 6 to 8 minutes per side, turning once, until cooked through — fish should feel firm when lightly pressed, and juices should run clear — and skin is crisp.
2 Sprinkle with coriander and serve with limes on the side.

Tau Yew Bak   Soy-braised Pork

Enormously satisfying in its rustic simplicity, this is the perfect dish to eat with rice congee.

2 tablespoon vegetable oil
2 tablespoons caster (superfine) sugar
600 g (1 lb 5^1/$_2$ oz) pork leg, skin on,
  cut into bite-sized chunks
6 cloves garlic, lightly crushed
625 ml (2^1/$_2$ cups) water
5 tablespoons thick dark soy sauce
^{1}/$_2$ teaspoon salt
a large walnut-sized knob of galangal,
  bruised

Serves 3–4
Cooking time: 1 hour 5 mins
Preparation time: 10 mins

1 Heat oil and sugar together in a wok over medium heat, stirring frequently. Watch it like a hawk; when sugar has melted and caramelized into little brown globules, add pork — caramel will splutter — and stir vigorously.
2 Add all remaining ingredients, bring to a boil, cover, and simmer for 1 hour, stirring occasionally, or until pork is fork tender. Serve hot.

Note Treacly thick dark soy sauce is the best to use for this dish, but if you cannot get it, use regular dark soy sauce.

Steamed Pomfret

There are two kinds of pomfret, of which the finer-fleshed white is better for this traditional Teochew dish. To make it more substantial, scatter thin slices of silken tofu and cooked dried Chinese mushrooms over and under the fish before steaming. Don't omit the lard — it makes a real difference to the fragrance.

1 large white pomfret, about 700 g (1 lb 9 oz), cleaned and gutted
1 tablespoon rendered pork lard
1 teaspoon light soy sauce
4 preserved sour plums
2 tablespoons finely shredded young ginger
1 large tomato, cut into 6 wedges
julienned spring onions, for garnish
chopped coriander leaves, for garnish

1 Score pomfret 2 to 3 times on each side and lay fish in heatproof serving dish. Drizzle lard and soy sauce over, and scatter plums, ginger, and tomato over the plate.
2 Steam fish, covered tightly, over high heat for 8 to 9 minutes or until fish is cooked through and juices have collected. Serve immediately, garnished with spring onions and fresh coriander.

Serves 2–4
Cooking time: 9 mins
Preparation time: 10 mins

ISAH MOHD YUSOF
CURRY SPICES
TEL : 2944320

Curries

The pundits think the word "curry" actually comes from the Tamil *kari*, which simply means "sauce"; or the Bengali *tarkari*, which means spiced stew; or even *kadhai*, which is the Tamil name for the wok-like Indian cooking pot. But over the last three centuries the word has come to mean any spiced, gravied dish. As convenient as it may be as a catch-all term, "curry" doesn't do any justice to the myriad Asian recipes that it attempts to refer to, which may be dry, moist, or wet, dark and pungent, pale and creamy, tear-inducingly hot or child-pleasingly mild … it's like describing classic Continental cuisine as "meat and sauce". But never mind the etymology: these are our favourite examples of this glorious "extended family" of foods.

Fish Moolie Deep-fried Fish in Spicy Coconut Sauce

Fried fish in a rich gravy that displays a blend of Indian and Malay influences. Any meaty fish will do.

1 whole red snapper or other firm-fleshed
  white fish, about 500 g (1 lb 2 oz)
1 teaspoon salt
Oil for deep-frying
3 tablespoons oil
330 ml (1 1/3 cups) coconut milk
1 tablespoon fish sauce
2 tablespoons shredded lime leaf
2 tomatoes, quartered
1 teaspoon sugar

Spice Paste
1 tablespoon shredded ginger
1 large onion
2 tablespoons ground coriander
1 tablespoon ground cumin
1 teaspoon chili powder

1 Clean and dry fish thoroughly. Rub with salt. Heat oil in a wok over medium heat until hazing, about 200°C (400°F), and deep-fry fish until crisp and golden brown, 3 to 4 minutes. Drain fish on kitchen paper.
2 Grind Spice Paste ingredients until fine. In a clean wok, heat 3 tablespoons fresh oil and fry Spice Paste over medium heat for 6 minutes, until thickened and fragrant.
3 Add coconut milk, fish sauce, half the lime leaf, tomatoes, and sugar and bring to a boil. Add fish and simmer 3 minutes, ladling sauce over fish and turning fish once. Turn over several times to coat liberally. Serve sprinkled with remaining lime leaf.

Serves 2–3
Prep time: 20 mins
Cooking time: 13 mins

Ikan Masak Pedas   Hot Fish Curry

A simple fish curry with a spicy kick — "pedas" means "hot" in Malay. Increase or reduce the chilies as you wish, for more or less pleasure!

600 g (1 lb 5$^1/_2$ oz) of any meaty fish, like
kurau or king fish cutlets
$^1/_2$ **teaspoon salt**
2$^1/_2$ tablespoons tamarind pulp
750 ml (3 cups) water
3 tablespoons vegetable oil
2 stalks lemongrass
1 teaspoon sugar
small handful shredded turmeric leaf
(_daun kunyit_)

Spice Paste
4 red chilies
3 dried chilies, soaked till soft
5 slices galangal
1 teaspoon chopped fresh turmeric
5 candlenuts
15 shallots
2 teaspoons shrimp paste

1 Slice fish into large chunks and rub with salt. Knead tamarind with water until pulp dissolves, then strain and set aside.
2 Grind all Spice Paste ingredients until very fine. Heat oil in a wok over medium-high heat and fry paste vigorously until fragrant, about 4 minutes. Add tamarind liquid, lemongrass, and sugar and bring to a boil, then add fish and simmer for 6 to 7 minutes or until fish is cooked. Garnish with turmeric leaf and serve.

Serves 2–4
Prep time: 20 mins
Cooking time: 10 mins

South Indian Fish Curry

Serve plenty of white rice on the side to soak up the sour, hot gravy. You can of course tone down the amount of chilies to taste. For more heft, add some sliced okra, brinjal, or tomatoes to the gravy with the fish.

2 tablespoons tamarind pulp
415 ml (1 $2/3$ cup) water
4 tablespoons oil
1 teaspoon black mustard seeds
1 stalk lemongrass, bruised
$3/4$ teaspoon salt
1 teaspoon sugar
600 g (1 lb 5 $1/2$ oz) mackerel steaks
1 sprig curry leaves

Spice Paste
2 tablespoons ground coriander
1 tablespoon ground cumin
$1/2$ teaspoon ground fennel
2 teaspoons chili powder
1 tablespoon chopped ginger
2 cloves garlic
4 shallots

1 Knead tamarind with water until pulp dissolves, then strain and set aside.
2 Grind Spice Paste ingredients until fine. Heat oil in a wok over medium heat, add Spice Paste and mustard seeds and fry until fragrant, 5 to 6 minutes.
3 Add tamarind liquid, lemongrass, salt, and sugar and bring to the boil. Simmer for 4 minutes, then add fish and curry leaves and simmer for 6 to 7 minutes more, until fish is cooked. Serve with white rice.

Serves 2–4
Prep time: 15 mins
Cooking time: 15 mins

Opor Ayam   Fragrant Coconut Chicken

Our rendition of an Indonesian coconut curry. It is slightly more complex than the original.

4 tablespoons vegetable oil
700 ml (2³/₄ cups plus 1 tablespoon)
  coconut milk
12 assorted chicken pieces, such as
  thighs, breasts, and drumsticks
3 dried chilies, soaked till soft
2 stalks lemongrass, bruised
4 lime leaves
1 teaspoon salt
1 teaspoon sugar

Spice Paste
3 slices galangal
3 slices ginger
5 candlenuts
12 shallots
1 thumb-size piece fresh turmeric
3 cloves garlic
1 tablespoon ground coriander
1 teaspoon ground cumin
¹/₂ teaspoon black pepper

1 Grind Spice Paste ingredients into a thick, fine paste. Heat oil in a wok over medium heat and fry Spice Paste for 6 minutes, until thickened and fragrant. Add 2 tablespoons coconut milk and fry for 2 minutes more.
2 Add chicken, chilies, lemongrass, lime leaves, and remaining coconut milk and simmer for 25 minutes.
3 Add salt and sugar, increase heat slightly and cook for 10 minutes more to thicken gravy slightly. Serve hot.

Note If you prefer the curry paler, leave out the turmeric. Grind the chilies with the Spice Paste if you want more heat. Chris prefers it subtle so he leaves them whole.

Serves 4–5
Prep time: 15 mins
Cooking time: 45 mins

Ayam Kurmah Aromatic Chicken

A Malay interpretation of an Indian *korma* that uses coconut milk instead of yoghurt or cream. This is very addictive with rice.

400 ml (1 3/5 cups) coconut milk
125 ml (1/2 cup) evaporated milk
4 tablespoons ground almonds
2 tablespoons lime juice
3 tablespoons vegetable ghee or oil
1 large onion, sliced
2 teaspoons minced ginger, pounded
  to a paste
6 cardamoms
6 cloves
2 stalks lemongrass, bruised
1 whole chicken, cut into 8–10 pieces
300 ml (1 cup plus 3 tablespoons) water
1 1/4 teaspoons salt
2 large potatoes, peeled and quartered
crisp-fried shallots, for garnish

Spice Paste
4 cloves garlic
6 candlenuts
2 tablespoons ground coriander
1 1/2 tablespoons ground cumin
1 teaspoon ground fennel
1 teaspoon fine black or white pepper
2 tablespoons water

1 Grind Spice Paste ingredients to a paste, adding a little more water if necessary if the paste is too stiff. Mix coconut milk, evaporated milk, ground almonds, and lime juice together, then set aside for 10 minutes so that it curdles slightly.
2 Heat ghee or oil in a wok over medium heat. Fry onion for 3 minutes or until soft, then add ginger, cardamoms, cloves, and lemongrass and spice paste. Fry for 5 to 6 minutes or until fragrant, stirring and scraping constantly to prevent scorching.
3 Add milk mixture, chicken, salt, and water and simmer for 30 minutes, then add potatoes and simmer for 20 minutes more. Garnish with plenty of crisp-fried shallots and serve.

Serves 3–4
Prep time: 15 mins plus 10 mins standing time
Cooking time: 1 hour

Ayam Lemak Puteh   White-cooked Chicken

A pale, aromatic dish. Serve with biryani rice or yellow rice cooked with ground turmeric.

1 chicken, about 1.2 kg ($^1/_2$ lb)
1 teaspoon salt
625 ml (2$^1/_2$ cups) coconut milk
100 ml ($^1/_3$ cup plus 1 tablespoon) water
4 tablespoons oil
2 stalks lemongrass, bruised
1 tablespoon fish sauce
juice of 1 lime

Spice Paste
150 g (5$^1/_4$ oz) onion
3 cloves garlic
2$^1/_2$ tablespoons minced galangal
2 tablespoons ground coriander
1 tablespoon ground cumin
1 teaspoon ground fennel
$^1/_2$ teaspoon white pepper

1 Cut chicken into 8 pieces and trim off any excess fat. Rub all over with salt.
2 Grind Spice Paste ingredients until very fine. Heat oil in a wok over medium heat and fry paste for 4 minutes, until thickened and fragrant. Add 2 tablespoons coconut milk and fry for 2 minutes more, stirring and scraping the wok constantly.
3 Add remaining coconut milk, water, lemongrass, and fish sauce and bring to the boil. Add chicken and simmer for 40 to 45 minutes or until chicken is tender and cooked through. Squeeze in lime juice and stir well before serving.

Serves 2–4
Prep time: 20 mins
Cooking time: 50 mins

Beef Rendang

An Indonesian curry, traditionally made with buffalo. It is up to you how much to reduce the sauce — you can cook it until the beef is bathed with a thick gravy — at which stage it is called *kalio* — or further until it is almost dry in true *rendang* style, in which case stir constantly near the end to prevent scorching.

1 kg (2$^1/_4$ lbs) rump or stewing steak,
  cut into large chunks
800 ml (3 cups + 3 tablespoons) coconut milk
3 stalks lemongrass
6 lime leaves
4 slices galangal
1 teaspoon salt

Spice Paste
5 tablespoons freshly grated coconut
8 dried chilies, soaked till soft
2 tablespoons ground coriander
1 tablespoon ground turmeric
1 teaspoon ground cumin
1 onion, chopped
1$^1/_2$ tablespoons minced ginger

1 To prepare the Spice Paste, fry coconut in a dry wok over medium-low heat, stirring constantly, until light brown, 5 to 6 minutes. Grind with remaining Spice Paste ingredients until fine.

2 Combine Spice Paste with all the beef and other ingredients in a large heavy-based pot and bring to a boil over medium heat. Reduce heat to low, partially cover and simmer for 1$^1/_2$ to 2 hours or until beef is tender and gravy is very thick and shiny with oil. Serve hot.

Note This keeps for a couple of weeks in the fridge, tightly covered. Use a clean spoon to dish out. It also freezes very well.

Serves 2–4
Prep time: 15 mins
Cooking time: 1$^3/_4$ to 2 hours

Devil Curry   Eurasian Spicy Mixed Meat Curry

Chris's version of a quintessential festive recipe from the Eurasian community, descendants of the Portuguese who sailed to Malacca in the 16th century. Very hot, very substantial, and irresistible. Also known as curry debal.

1 large chicken, cut into serving portions
1 tablespoon light soy sauce
1 tablespoon dark soy sauce
30 dried chilies, soaked until soft
3 stalks lemongrass, thinly sliced
8 garlic cloves, peeled
3 red onions, peeled
3 tablespoons chopped fresh galangal
2 teaspoons chopped fresh turmeric
125 ml ($^1/_2$ cup) cooking oil
4 tablespoons shredded ginger
2 teaspoons black mustard seeds
2 large onions, peeled and quartered
6 tomatoes, quartered
750 ml (3 cups) water
250 g (9 oz) Chinese roast pork with
    crackling (*siew yok*), cut into chunks
4 smoked sausages (such as *bockwurst*),
    cut into chunks
3 tablespoons English mustard
75 ml ($^1/_3$ cup) vinegar
$^1/_2$ white cabbage, cut into large pieces
salt, to taste
sugar, to taste

Topping
2 tablespoons oil
1 large onion, sliced
2 red chilies, sliced diagonally
3 tablespoons shredded ginger

1 Toss chicken with soy sauces to coat, then place in an oiled roasting tin and roast for 40 minutes in a preheated oven at 190°C (375°F).
2 Grind soaked chilies to a paste with lemongrass and garlic and set aside. Grind red onions, galangal, and turmeric together into a paste and set aside.
3 Heat oil in a large wok over medium-low heat. When hot, add chili paste and fry, stirring constantly, 8 to 10 minutes or until slightly darkened and "raw" smell has dissipated. Spoon paste into a bowl, leaving oil in pan. Add onion paste, ginger, and mustard seeds to pan and fry 6 to 7 minutes, stirring constantly, until thick and fragrant.
4 Return chili paste to wok and fry 1 minute more, then add chicken with juices and browned bits in roasting tin, onions, tomatoes, and water. Bring to a boil and simmer for 15 minutes, then add the roast pork, smoked sausage, mustard, and vinegar. Simmer 15 minutes more, then add cabbage. Cook 6 to 8 minutes or until cabbage is tender, then season with salt and sugar to taste.
5 To make Topping, heat oil over high heat, then add onions, chilies, and ginger and toss until lightly browned, 2 to 3 minutes. Sprinkle over curry to serve.

Note Add some bacon bones in step 4 to make this even more authentic, and calorific. Once fully cooled, store in an airtight container in the fridge, where it will keep for at least a week. Remove what you want to eat with a clean spoon and bring to a full boil before serving.

Serves 6–7
Prep time: 30 mins
Cooking time: 1 hour 45 minutes

Peranakan Classics

The importance of food to the Peranakans cannot be overstated. Along with our wedding customs, traditional dress and jewellery, lingo — a unique version of Malay spiced up with words borrowed from Chinese dialects — and music, it is one of the key distinctives of the culture. However, Peranakan cuisine is still not as well known outside of Asia as it deserves to be, though perhaps the current global popularity of Thai food will prime the pump for a Peranakan craze. We certainly hope so.

Here is but a small subset of all our favourites, but we hope it makes a good introduction to Peranakan food if you have never experienced it before.

Nasi Ulam   Herbal Rice Salad

The Peranakans of Kelantan, Malaysia, are known for their variations on this cold rice salad, which may contain up to 15 herbs, including the quirkily-named *daun kentut* or flatulence leaf.

2 whole *ikan selar* (yellowstripe trevally),
   or other fine-fleshed white fish, about
   450 g (1 lb)
6 tablespoons vegetable oil
6 shallots, thinly sliced
4 cloves garlic, thinly sliced
200 g (7 oz) fresh grated coconut
4 long beans
$^1/_2$ cucumber, peeled and deseeded
2 stalks lemongrass
4 lime leaves (*daun limau purut*)
small handful basil leaves (*daun kemangi*
   or *daun selaseh*)
small handful laksa leaves (*daun kesom*)
small handful mint leaves (*daun pudina*)
1 turmeric leaf (*daun kunyit*)
1 teaspoon fine sea salt
600 g (1 lb 5$^1/_2$ oz) cold cooked rice
Sambal Blachan (p. 25) , to serve

1 Clean fish and pat dry. Cook under a hot grill for 10 minutes, turning once. Let cool completely, then skin and debone. Flake flesh finely. Cool and flake.
2 Heat oil in a wok over medium heat and fry sliced shallots and garlic until light brown, 3 to 4 minutes. Drain on kitchen paper.
3 In a clean wok over low heat, dry-fry coconut for 6 to 8 minutes, stirring constantly, until golden brown.
4 Slice long beans very thinly and finely dice cucumber. Slice lemongrass as thinly as you can with a very sharp knife. Shred all herbs finely. Toss all ingredients together with rice until thoroughly mixed. Serve immediately with Sambal Blachan (p. 25) on the side.

Serves 4–5
Cooking time: 25 mins
Preparation time: 30 mins

Kuah Lada   Peppery Fish Curry

Peppery, sour, and very appetite-stimulating.

2 tablespoons tamarind pulp
625 ml (2¹/₂ cups) water
4 tablespoons vegetable oil
1 teaspoon salt
1 teaspoon sugar
500 g (1 lb 2 oz) stingray or baby shark
2 brinjals, cut into large batons
2 stalks lemongrass, bruised

Spice Paste
3 red chilies
6 candlenuts
10 shallots
1 thumb-sized piece fresh turmeric
1 teaspoon black peppercorns
3 slices galangal

1 Grind Spice Paste ingredients fine. Cut fish into large pieces.
2 Knead tamarind pulp with half of the water until dissolved. Strain and mix with remaining water.
3 Heat oil in a wok and fry Spice Paste over medium heat for 6 minutes, until fragrant. Transfer to a pot and add tamarind liquid, salt, and sugar. Bring to the boil and add fish, brinjals, and lemongrass, then simmer for 10 to 12 minutes, until fish is cooked. Serve hot with rice.

Serves 4–5
Cooking time: 20 mins
Preparation time: 15 mins

Bakwan Kepiting   Stuffed Crab and Pork Ball Soup

"*Bakwan*" means Hokkien for meatball, and "*kepiting*" is Malay for crab. In his university days, Chris made this with canned crabmeat with great success.

6 large mottled crabs, washed
3 tablespoons vegetable oil
6 cloves garlic, chopped
75 g (2 3/4 oz) bamboo shoots, finely
  sliced
250 g (9 oz) minced pork
2 tablespoons finely chopped fresh
  coriander
1 teaspoon salt
1/2 teaspoon white pepper
2 tablespoons light soy sauce
1 1/2 liters (6 cups) water or light
  pork stock

Serves 6
Cooking time: 15 mins
Preparation time: 20 mins

1 Bring a large pot of water to the boil over high heat, add crabs, return to the boil and simmer for 6 minutes. Drain crabs and when cool, remove all meat and roe (if any), discarding lungs and fibrous tissue. Reserve body shells.
2 Heat oil over medium heat and fry garlic until light brown, 2 to 3 minutes. Mix half the garlic and its oil, crabmeat, crab roe, half the bamboo shoots, minced pork, coriander, salt, pepper, and half the soy sauce together.
3 Stuff each shell with the crab mixture. Shape remaining stuffing into small balls. Bring water or stock to a boil and slip in stuffed shells and balls. Simmer for 5 to 6 minutes or until cooked through. Stir in remaining bamboo shoots, garlic, and soy sauce. Serve hot, garnished with fresh coriander.

Rebong Lemak   Pork Ribs and Bamboo Shoot Curry

The bamboo gives this very cross-cultural dish a distinctive flavour and crunch.

3 tablespoons vegetable oil
600 g (1 lb 5¹/₂ oz) pork ribs, cut into
   5-cm (2 in) chunks
200 g (7 oz) bamboo shoots, sliced
625 ml (2¹/₂ cups) coconut milk
1 teaspoon salt
1 teaspoon sugar

Spice Paste
8 dried chilies, soaked till soft
2 stalks 3 thin slices galangal
1 tablespoon shrimp paste
1 thumb-sized piece of fresh turmeric
2 tablespoons ground coriander
1 teaspoon black pepper

1 Grind all Spice Paste ingredients until fine.
2 Heat oil in wok over medium-low heat and fry paste, stirring constantly, until thickened and fragrant, 6 to 8 minutes.
3 Add all other ingredients to wok, bring to a boil and simmer over medium-low heat, partially covered, for 45 minutes or until ribs are very tender. Serve hot.

Serves 3–4
Cooking time: 50 mins
Preparation time: 10 mins

Rinse canned bamboo shoots well before use.

Babi Assam Tamarind-braised Pork

Traditionally made with belly pork, but you can use any cut, as long as it includes a little fat — essential for the best flavor and texture. This keeps, tightly covered, in the fridge for at least a week. It never lasts any longer in our house.

$2^1/_2$ tablespoons tamarind pulp
425 ml ($1^2/_3$ cups) water
5 tablespoons oil
1 tablespoon preserved yellow beans
  (*tau cheo*), mashed
650 g ($1^1/_2$ lbs) pork rib-eye, cubed
2 stalks lemongrass, bruised
3 tablespoons palm sugar
salt to taste
$^1/_2$ ginger bud (*bunga kantan*), shredded

Spice Paste
10 shallots
4 candlenuts (*buah keras*)
3 tablespoons chopped galangal
3 cloves garlic
1 thumb-sized piece fresh turmeric
1 tablespoon chopped ginger
2 dried chilies
4 fresh red chilies
1 teaspoon shrimp paste

1 Knead tamarind with water until pulp dissolves, then strain and set aside.
2 Grind all Spice Paste ingredients together until fine. Heat oil in a wok over medium heat and fry paste, stirring constantly, for 6 to 8 minutes or until paste is fragrant and has reduced in volume by about $^1/_3$.
3 Add yellow beans and fry 1 minute, then add pork, lemongrass, and tamarind liquid and stir well. Simmer for 1 hour, partially covered, until pork is tender and gravy has thickened. Stir in palm sugar and salt to taste. Garnish with ginger bud and serve hot with rice.

Serves 4–5
Cooking time: 1 hour 10 mins
Preparation time: 15 mins

Itek Sio   Braised Duck in Tamarind and Coriander

Deceptively simple, this does take time but is well worth the effort; the important thing is to cook it long and slow until the duck is fork-tender and the sauce aromatic and glossy. Traditionally sweetened with bruised lengths of sugar cane, but muscovado sugar gives the same flavor with less effort.

1 cleaned duck, about 2$^1/_2$ kg (5$^1/_2$ lbs)
3 tablespoons ground coriander
1$^1/_2$ teaspoons salt
2 teaspoon black pepper
2 tablespoons light muscovado or
    raw sugar
4 tablespoons dark soy sauce
1 tablespoon tamarind pulp
190 ml ($^3/_4$ cup) water
4 tablespoons oil
250 g (9 oz) onions, very finely minced
3 liters (12 cups) water
2 cinnamon sticks
8 cloves
4 tablespoons chopped fresh coriander
    leaves

1 Clean duck thoroughly and wipe dry. Mix salt, coriander, pepper, sugar, and soy sauce together and rub all over duck. Let marinate for 1 hour at room temperature. Knead tamarind with water until pulp dissolves, strain and set aside.

2 Heat oil in a large wok over medium heat and fry onions until soft and light brown, 6 to 8 minutes. Put in duck and fry, turning constantly, to brown skin all over.

3 Add tamarind liquid, water, cinnamon, and cloves and bring to a gentle boil. Simmer, covered, for about 2$^1/_2$ hours or until duck is very tender, turning duck 2 or 3 times and topping up with more water if necessary. Transfer duck to a chopping board and let rest for 10 minutes. Meanwhile, turn heat to high and reduce sauce until thickened and glossy.

4 Chop duck into serving pieces. Arrange these on serving plate, pour some sauce over, and sprinkle with chopped coriander. Serve extra sauce on the side.

Serves 4–6
Cooking time: 3 hours
Preparation time: 10 mins + 1 hour marinating time

An unlikely blend of flavors, you might think, but the tangy, meaty, aromatic result is immensely comforting on a cold day.

1 duck, cleaned and cut into 8 pieces
1^1/$_2$ liters (6 cups) water
200 g (7 oz) pork leg, cut into chunks
400 g (14^1/$_4$ oz) salted vegetable
4 preserved sour plums
3 tomatoes, quartered
1 teaspoon sugar
4 green chilies
2 tablespoons brandy or cognac

Serves 4–6
Cooking time: 1^1/$_2$ hours
Preparation time: 10 mins

1 Trim off any excess fat from duck and place in a large pot with pork leg and water. Bring to the boil and cook for 1^1/$_4$ hours or until meats are very tender.
2 Slice salted vegetable into large pieces and add to pot with sour plums, tomatoes, and sugar. Simmer, covered, for 10 minutes more. Skim off as much oil as you can from the surface.
3 Break green chilies into small pieces with your fingers and stir in with brandy. Serve hot.

Note Save time by using a pressure cooker to simmer duck and pork for 30 minutes, before continuing with step 2, cooking uncovered.

Nangka Lemak Young Jackfruit Curry

Sold in bags by Malay vegetable stalls, unripe jackfruit or *nangka* is pale green, firm, and astringent. As it ripens it turns yellow and becomes more easy to separate into lobes of crisp-textured flesh.

1 kg (2$\frac{1}{4}$ lbs) unripe *nangka*, skin discarded
1 teaspoon salt
4 tablespoons vegetable oil
625 ml (2$\frac{1}{2}$ cups) coconut milk
200 g (7 oz) fresh shrimps, shelled
2 tablespoons fish sauce
2 teaspoons sugar

Spice Paste
3 tablespoons dried shrimps, soaked in warm water till soft
2 stalks lemongrass
8 red chilies
6 candlenuts
1 large onion
1 tablespoon shrimp paste
1 thumb-size piece fresh turmeric

1 Slice *nangka* into large chunks. Bring a large pot of water to the boil. Add *nangka* and salt and simmer for 15 minutes or until the fruit is tender. Drain and rinse *nangka* with cold water. Set aside.

2 Grind Spice Paste ingredients until fine. Heat oil in a wok over medium heat and fry paste for about 6 minutes, until thickened and fragrant. Add coconut milk and *nangka* and simmer for 7 to 8 minutes.

3 Add shrimps and cook for 2 minutes. Stir in fish sauce and sugar. Serve hot with rice.

Serves 4–6
Cooking time: 30 mins
Preparation time: 20 mins

Malay stalls sell cubed unripe *nangka*.

Babi Chin   Sweet Pork

There are several cultures in this sweet, aromatic dish, Indian, Chinese, and Thai principally. If you have time, dry-roast coriander seeds till fragrant and grind them fresh for this dish — it really makes a difference.

2 heaped tablespoons ground coriander
2 tablespoons cold water
4 tablespoons vegetable oil
15 shallots, finely minced
8 cloves garlic, finely minced
3 tablespoons preserved yellow beans
  (*tau cheo*), mashed
500 g (1 lb 2 oz) pork shoulder, cut into
  large chunks
3 tablespoons thick, dark soy sauce
1 teaspoon salt
1¹/₂ tablespoons sugar
¹/₂ teaspoon ground cinnamon
¹/₂ teaspoon ground cloves
1 liter (4 cups) water
150 g (5¹/₄ oz) bamboo shoots, cut into
  small pieces
3–4 fresh green chilies

1 Mix ground coriander with water to make a wet paste.
2 Heat oil in a wok over medium heat and fry shallots for 3 minutes, stirring constantly, then add garlic and fry for 2 minutes more. Add coriander paste and mashed yellow beans. Stir well for 2 minutes.
3 Add pork, thick soy sauce, salt, sugar, cinnamon, cloves, and water and transfer to a pot. Simmer for 30 minutes. Add bamboo shoots and simmer 10 minutes more, until gravy is thick and aromatic. Break green chilies into rough pieces and mix in, then serve immediately.

Serves 4–6
Cooking time: 45 mins
Preparation time: 15 mins

Sambal Babi Spiced Pork

Very moreish and as good in a sandwich as it is with white rice. This keeps well, refrigerated and covered airtight, and in fact tastes better the next day.

1¹/₂ kg (3¹/₄ lbs) belly pork, skin removed
4 tablespoons vegetable oil
1 teaspoon salt
1 tablespoon sugar
2 tablespoons dark soy sauce
4 lime leaves, shredded (optional)

Spice Paste
6 cloves garlic
200 g (7 oz) large onions or shallots
8 candlenuts
2 stalks lemongrass
4 slices of galangal
6–8 dried chilies, soaked till soft
1 tablespoon shrimp paste

1 Slice belly pork thickly. Blanch slices in a large pot of boiling water for 8 minutes, then drain well and cut into bite-sized chunks.
2 Grind all Spice Paste ingredients until fine. Heat oil in a wok over medium-low heat and fry the paste until thickened and fragrant, 7 to 8 minutes.
3 Add pork, sugar, salt, and soy sauce, reduce heat to low and fry for 15 minutes, stirring constantly. Add a little water as necessary to prevent pork from scorching. When done, pork should be tender and coated with very thick sauce. until well incorporated. Mix in shredded lime leaves before serving.

Serves 4–5
Cooking time: 30 mins
Preparation time: 15 mins

Satay Babi Goreng   Fried Pork Satay

This is a pan-fried variation of skewered satay given a fragrant twist by Nonya cooks with the infusion of lime leaves.

600 g (1 lb 5$^1/_2$ oz) pork rib steak, marbled with a little fat
415 ml (1$^2/_3$ cups) coconut milk
4 lime leaves
1 teaspoon salt
2 teaspoons sugar

Spice Paste
3 stalks, use 5 cm (2 in) of root end
5 fresh red chilies
5 candlenuts
10 shallots
1 tablespoon shrimp paste
1 teaspoon turmeric powder
2 tablespoons coriander powder
1 teaspoon cumin powder
1 teaspoon fennel powder

1 Cut pork into thin slices. Grind Spice Paste ingredients, except the powders, and mix into a thick paste with a little water.
2 Heat oil and fry Spice Paste for 4 minutes until fragrant and oil oozes out. Add pork and continue to fry for 3 minutes.
3 Add coconut milk, lime leaves, salt, and sugar and boil over medium heat stirring constantly until gravy is thick and aromatic.

Serves 4
Cooking time: 35 minutes

Desserts

With four official cultures and countless subcultures to draw on, not to mention the fertile ground where Asian flavours meet Western dessert techniques, picking typical Singaporean desserts for this book wasn't an easy prospect. And mind you, Terry hardly ever eats dessert! But after racking my brain and my files, I plumped for the sweets that I hanker for most after a season of healthy eating. All are traditional — even the pandan chiffon, which debuted locally over 30 years ago — and some, like the *kueh tart* and the *apom bekuah*, are truly fit for grand occasions.

Pineapple Tarts   Kueh Tart

These rich Chinese New Year delicacies may originally have Portuguese origins, but are now very ecumenical; in Malacca, the Nonya, Eurasian, Chitty, and Malay communities all make different versions. Rather than the traditional grated fresh pineapple, I prefer to use canned pineapple in natural juice as it is consistently ripe and flavorful.

Pineapple Jam
4 cans (about 500 g or 1 lb 2 oz each)
   pineapple chunks in natural juice
1 whole star anise, broken into petals
3 cinnamon sticks
7 cloves
450 g (1 lb) caster sugar, plus more
   as necessary

Pastry
400 g (14 oz) plain flour, sifted
2 tablespoons caster sugar
$2/3$ teaspoon salt
250 g (9 oz) cold unsalted butter, cubed
3 egg yolks
2 teaspoons vanilla extract
50 ml (scant $1/4$ cup) iced water
1 egg, beaten with 1 tablespoon water

Tart
1 egg, beaten with 1 tablespoon water
whole cloves

Makes 5 to 6 dozen tarts
Cooking time: 2 hrs + 20 mins baking time
  (per batch)
Preparation time: 45 mins per batch +
  20 mins chilling time.

1 To make the Pineapple Jam, drain pineapple, reserving juice, and chop it very finely in a food processor. Combine with juice, spices, and sugar in a large, wide pot (non-aluminum, preferably non-stick). Stir well over medium heat until sugar dissolves. Taste, then add more sugar as necessary for a good tart-sweet balance.

2 Bring to a boil, then reduce heat to medium-low and cook, stirring very frequently, until the mixture is reduced to a thick, amber-colored jam, $1^1/_2$ to $2^1/_2$ hours. Watch it carefully towards the end of cooking, stirring constantly to prevent scorching. Let cool competely. Store in clean airtight jars or plastic containers in the fridge.

3 To make Pastry, whisk flour, sugar, and salt together in a large mixing bowl until well blended. Add butter cubes and rub them in with your fingertips or a pastry blender, until the mixture resembles fine breadcrumbs. Whisk egg yolks, vanilla, and water together and drizzle evenly over flour mixture. Stir with a fork to bring dough together into a ball. Knead lightly for 5 seconds, then divide into three portions. Wrap in plastic wrap and chill for 1 hour.

4 Repeat Step 3 with fresh ingredients to make additional pastry. You will need at least two batches of Pastry (quantities given make one batch) to use up the jam. Make one batch at a time to avoid over-mixing.

5 To make Tarts, work with and bake one third of a pastry batch at a time. Pinch off a large walnut-sized piece of pastry and flatten it about 4 mm (generous 1/8 in) thick with your fingers. Place 1 teaspoon of jam on pastry and bring up edges to enclose. Pinch off excess pastry and roll ball between palms to make it evenly round. Brush tart with beaten egg to glaze and stick a clove into it. If you like, use a small pair of scissors to snip tiny 'v's in the pastry to make tart resemble a pineapple. Repeat Step 5 with remaining pastry and jam.

6 Place tarts on a baking sheet lines with baking paper and bake in a pre-heated oven at 170°C (340°F) for 20 to 25 minutes or until golden brown. If tarts brown too fast, lower heat to 160°C (320°F) halfway through. When done, cool on a rack before storing airtight.

Apom Bekuah   Coconut Pancakes with Banana Sauce

This has Indonesian and Peranakan roots. The contrast of light, spongy pancakes with a rich banana sauce is irresistible. Use a creamy-textured banana type for good results.

Pancakes
250 g (9 oz) rice flour
75 ml ($^1/_3$ cup) water
300 ml (1 cup plus 3 tablespoons) coconut
  water, or plain water mixed with 2 teaspoons sugar
2$^1/_4$ teaspoons active dried yeast
1 tablespoon sugar
3 tablespoons cake flour
2 tablespoons glutinous rice flour
$^3/_4$ teaspoon salt
150 ml ($^2/_3$ cup) coconut milk
vegetable oil
2 tablespoons *bunga telang* juice (optional)
  See Glossary)

Sauce
100 g (3$^1/_2$ oz) *gula melaka* (palm sugar)
3 tablespoons caster (superfine) sugar
100 ml ($^1/_3$ cup plus 1 tablespoon) water
2 pandan leaves, knotted
300 ml (1 cup plus 3 tablespoons)
  coconut milk
2 teaspoons glutinous rice flour, dissolved
  in 2 tablespoons water
$^1/_2$ teaspoon salt
5 bananas, sliced

1 Stir 2 tablespoons of the rice flour and 75 ml ($^1/_3$ cup) water together over low heat, until mixture thickens to a paste. Transfer to a large mixing bowl and whisk in remaining rice flour, coconut water, yeast, sugar, cake flour, and glutinous rice flour. Let stand at cool room temperature for 2 hours or until frothy and doubled in volume.

2 Whisk in coconut milk and let stand 1 more hour.

3 Lightly stir batter. Heat an *apom bekuah* pan over medium-low heat (preferably on a wide burner). Grease depressions with oil. When hot, ladle a scant 2 tablespoons plain batter into each depression — batter should sizzle — then swirl in a drop of *bunga telang* juice. Cover and cook for 5 to 6 minutes, or until pancakes are browned on the bottom. Transfer cooked pancakes to a plate. You should get 20 to 22 *apom bekuah* pancakes in total.

4 To make Sauce, bring *gula melaka*, caster sugar, water, and pandan leaves to a boil in a pot over medium heat, stirring to dissolve sugars. Add coconut milk, glutinous rice flour paste, salt, and bananas and cook, stirring occasionally, for 6 minutes or until bananas are just tender. Serve hot with pancakes.

Note *Apom bekuah* pans have four to six saucer-shaped depressions just under 1 cm ($^1/_2$ in) deep and about 6 to 7 cm (about 3 in) across. If you cannot find one, use small crumpet rings — the batter is too thin to be fried as for normal pancakes.

Serves 5–6
Cooking time: 40 mins (approx)
Preparation time: 10 mins + 3 hours standing time

Payasam   Indian Rice Pudding with Cashews and Raisins

A *payasam* is a milk-based dessert of which there are many variations, hailing from all over India. This one is thickened with rice. You can substitute jaggery (Indian palm sugar) for half the sugar for a caramel-like flavor.

1 liter (4 cups) full-cream milk
90 g (3 oz) basmati rice, rinsed and
  drained
3 cardamom pods, lightly crushed
$1/_4$ teaspoon ground nutmeg
100 g ($3^1/_2$ oz) sugar
2 tablespoons ghee or butter
100 g ($3^1/_2$ oz) raw cashew nuts
4 tablespoons raisins
pinch ground cardamom, for garnish if
  desired

Serves 4–5
Cooking time: 50 mins
Preparation time: 5 mins

1 Over medium heat, bring milk to the boil in a large heavy-based saucepan, stirring occasionally. Add rice, cardamom, and nutmeg and return to the boil. Reduce heat to low and cook, partially covered, for about 40 minutes or until rice is soft, stirring frequently.

2 When rice is done, stir in sugar until dissolved. Switch off heat, cover and set aside.

3 Melt ghee in a small frying pan over medium-low heat. Add cashew nuts and raisins and fry until nuts are lightly browned, 4 to 5 minutes. Stir nuts and raisins into *payasam*, reserving a few for garnish. Serve *payasam* hot or cold, garnished with reserved nuts, raisins, and a sprinkle of ground cardamom if desired.

Kueh Dadar   Coconut-stuffed Pandan Pancake Rolls

A little bit of untraditional baking powder helps to make softer, lighter pancakes. These do not keep well and are best eaten fresh.

Pancakes
100 g (3¹/₂ oz) cake flour, sifted
100 g (3¹/₂ oz) plain flour, sifted
1¹/₂ tablespoons caster (superfine) sugar
¹/₂ teaspoon salt
425 ml (1²/₃ cups) coconut milk
5 tablespoons Pandan Juice (see Note)
1 large egg
¹/₂ teaspoon baking powder

Filling
175 g (6¹/₂ oz) palm sugar, finely chopped
4 tablespoons caster (superfine) sugar
80 ml (¹/₃ cup) water
2 pandan leaves, knotted
¹/₃ teaspoon salt
250 g (9 oz) fresh grated coconut

Makes 20 *kueh dadar*
Cooking time: 40 mins
Preparation time: 15 mins + 15 mins
   standing time

1 To make Filling, combine palm and caster sugars, water, pandan leaves, and salt in a saucepan and stir over low heat until sugars have dissolved. Strain into a clean pan and add coconut. Cook, stirring constantly, over medium-low heat for 5 to 7 minutes, or until coconut has absorbed all the liquid and formed moist, juicy clumps. Set aside to cool.
2 Combine cake and plain flours, sugar, and salt in a mixing bowl. Whisk coconut milk, Pandan Juice, and egg together and slowly whisk into flour mixture, beating only until smooth. Let batter stand for 15 minutes at room temperature. Whisk in baking powder just before you begin to fry the pancakes.
3 Lightly grease a non-stick frying pan and set it over medium-low heat. Spoon 2 to 3 tablespoons of batter into pan and tilt pan to spread batter into a thin pancake. Cook 45 seconds or until edges look dry, then flip and cook 40 seconds more or until set and cooked. Transfer to plate and repeat with remaining batter. Pancakes should blister but barely color, if at all.
4 To assemble *kueh*, lay a pancake on a plate. Stir filling and place 1 tablespoon near a pancake edge, then roll up from that edge, tucking in the sides as you go, as you would make a spring roll. Repeat with remaining filling and pancakes.

Note To make Pandan Juice, chop 40 to 50 pandan leaves into short lengths. Place in a food processor or mini-chopper with 2 tablespoons water and blend to a grassy pulp. Place pulp in a fine sieve or a muslin bag and squeeze for deep green juice.

Sago Gula Melaka   Sago Pearl Pudding with Palm Sugar

Easily made, easily multiplied, and therefore a good party dessert. Make sure all ingredients are best quality.

130 g (4$^1/_2$ oz) sago pearls
3 liters (12 cups) water

Sauces
200 g (7 oz) palm sugar, chopped
100 ml ($^1/_3$ cup plus 1 tablespoon) water
250 ml (1 cup) coconut milk
$^1/_4$ teaspoon salt

Serves 4–5
Cooking time: 15 mins
Preparation time: 10 mins + 1 hr standing time

1 Rinse sago pearls, transfer to a large bowl, and cover with plenty of cold water. Let soak 15 minutes.
2 Bring 3 liters (12 cups) water to boil in a large pot. Drain sago and add to pot. Return water to the boil and simmer steadily for 8 to 9 minutes or until pearls are almost fully translucent, with just the barest white fleck in the center of each (they will continue to cook off the heat — boiling them until fully translucent makes them mushy).
3 Pour contents of pot into a large fine-meshed sieve and shake to drain off excess water. Working quickly, spoon pearls into 4 or 5 individual moulds, cups or ramekins, pressing lightly to pack them in. Let cool, then chill for 45 minutes or until fully set.
4 Combine chopped *gula melaka* with water in a small pot and cook over medium heat until smooth. Strain into a serving jug. In a clean pot, bring coconut milk to the boil with the salt. Simmer 1 minute, then pour into another serving jug and let cool. Serve sago puddings cold with the two sauces.

Foo Chok Pak Kor   Sweet Beancurd Skin and Gingko Nut Dessert Soup

A traditional Chinese sweet soup, or "*tong sui,*" that has cooling properties. Chilled, it makes an excellent, nourishing hot-weather dessert.

50 g (1³/₄ oz) pearl barley
1¹/₂ liters (6 cups) water
1 sheet dried beancurd skin (*foo chok*),
  about 35–40 g
90 g (3 oz) rock sugar, broken up
100 g (3¹/₂ oz) prepared ginkgo nuts
2 egg whites (optional)

Serves 3–4
Cooing time: 1¹/₄ hours
Preparation time: 5 minutes

1 Combine barley and 1 liter (4 cups) water in a saucepan and bring to the boil. Partially cover, reduce heat and simmer gently for 50 minutes, or until barley is tender and liquid has reduced by about half.
2 Meanwhile, rinse beancurd skin with warm water to remove traces of oil. Tear it into large pieces.
3 Add remaining 500 ml (2 cups) water, rock sugar, ginkgo nuts, and bean-curd skin to pot and simmer, uncovered, for 10 minutes more.
4 If desired, beat egg whites until well mixed, then slowly drizzle into pot in a thin stream, stirring as you pour so the whites form thin strands. Serve hot or cold.

Note You can adjust the thickness of the dessert by increasing or reducing the amount of barley.

Cheng Thng · Sweet Clear Dessert Soup

Every Chinese family has a different recipe for this classic sweet dessert soup.

20 prepared or canned lotus seeds
20 prepared or canned ginkgo nuts
1 small head white fungus (*shuit yee*)
2 dried persimmons
12 whole dried longans
1 liter (4 cups) water
2 pandan leaves, knotted
150 g (5¹/₄ oz) rock sugar
1 tablespoon granulated sugar

Serves 4
Cooking time: 20 mins
Preparation time: 15 mins

1 Drain lotus seeds and gingko nuts and rinse under cold tap. Soak white fungus in cold water for 15 minutes or until swollen.
2 Rinse dried persimmons and slice into 1-cm (¹/₂-in) strips, removing the hard tip. Remove longan shells and stones and rinse meat.
3 Bring water to the boil in a large pot and add knotted pandan leaves, rock sugar, granulated sugar, longan meat, and dried persimmon. Simmer gently for 10 minutes.
4 Add lotus seeds, ginkgo nuts, and white fungus and simmer for 5 minutes. Remove pandan leaves. Serve hot, or let cool completely and serve over crushed ice.

Dried white fungus cooks up translucent.

Bubur Terigu White Wheat Pudding with Palm Sugar and Coconut Milk

A hearty porridge of wheat kernels and coconut milk that is best served warm, on a cool day. It does not keep well. Terry has a hypothesis that this has Indian origins, as "*terigu*" seems to be a corruption of "Telegu," where this wheat is grown.

300 g (10¹/₂ oz) *terigu* (white
  wheat kernels)
2 pandan leaves, knotted
3 liters (12 cups) water
275 ml (1 cup plus 2 tablespoons)
  coconut milk

Syrup
200 g (7 oz) palm sugar, chopped
4 tablespoons caster (superfine) sugar
165 ml (²/₃ cup) water
¹/₂ teaspoon salt

Topping
100 ml (¹/₃ cup plus 1 tablespoon)
  coconut milk
¹/₄ teaspoon salt

1 Rinse wheat to remove stray grit or dirt. Cover with cold water and let soak 15 minutes.
2 Drain wheat well and combine with pandan leaves and 3 liters (12 cups) fresh water in a large pot. Bring to a boil, then reduce heat to medium-low, partially cover, and simmer, stirring occasionally, for 2 hours, or until the grains have absorbed most of the water and are soft, but still have a slight bite to them. Add more or less water for thicker or thinner texture, as you desire.
3 While wheat cooks, combine Syrup ingredients and stir over low heat until sugars dissolve. When wheat is done, add sugar syrup to pot and cook 5 minutes, then add coconut milk. Cook, stirring, until mixture is just about to boil, then switch off heat.
4 To make Topping, bring coconut milk to a boil with salt in a small pot over medium heat. Simmer 1 minute, then pour into a bowl and cool. Serve *bubur terigu*, with topping on the side for people to help themselves.

Serves 4–5
Cooking time: 2 ¹/₄ hours
Preparation time: 15 mins

Pandan Chiffon Cake

Asian pandan leaves and coconut milk infuse the American-invented chiffon cake with a happy marriage of flavors. A time-honored Singaporean party staple, often purchased nowadays but vastly better home-made.

60 pandan leaves
75 ml (1/4 cup) plus 1 tablespoon thick coconut milk
7 egg yolks
125 ml (1/2 cup) vegetable oil
225 g (8 oz) cake flour (such as Softasilk)
300 g (10 1/2 oz) sugar
1 1/2 teaspoons baking powder
1/2 teaspoon salt
8 egg whites
1 teaspoon cream of tartar

Serves 8–10
Cooking time: 1 hour
Preparation time: 20 mins

1 Preheat oven to 165°C (325°F). Have ready a dry, ungreased 23-cm (9-in) round chiffon cake pan.
2 Snip pandan leaves into short lengths with scissors, then blend in a mini-chopper or food processor for a few minutes, until reduced to a grassy pulp. Transfer pulp to a muslin bag or fine sieve and squeeze for juice. Measure out 115 ml of juice (if not enough, make up difference with water) into a bowl, add coconut milk, egg yolks, and vegetable oil and whisk until smooth. Set aside.
3 Sift cake flour into a large bowl. Add all but 3 tablespoons of the sugar, baking powder, and salt and whisk well to blend, then add egg yolk mixture and whisk until smooth.
4 In a clean, grease-free bowl, beat egg whites with cream of tartar at high speed until soft peaks form. Gradually beat in remaining 3 tablespoons of sugar, beating just until stiff peaks start to form. Fold egg whites into batter in three additions, folding just until incorporated (a few thin white streaks are okay). Pour batter into pan, level surface with spatula, and bake for 55 to 60 minutes. Cake is done when an inserted thin skewer comes out clean.
5 Invert cake onto a rack and leave to cool upside down in the pan. Cut around edge and base with a thin-bladed knife to release cake from pan. Slice to serve.

Choose springy, dark green pandan leaves.

Chop them, then blend to a grassy pulp.

Squeeze pulp in muslin for green juice.

Ingredients

Assam gelugor (*assam keping*) is a sour-sweet fruit, sold dried in slices that resemble dried apple; not related to tamarind pods.

Bamboo shoot is a staple ingredient throughout Asia and is available fresh, dried, brined, or pickled.

Banana leaf is used to wrap savory or sweet dishes before steaming or grilling, as it imparts a wonderful fragrance.

Bangkwang (yam bean or jicama) is a root vegetable with sweet, crunchy white flesh. It is eaten raw in *rojak* or cooked for *popiah* (fresh spring roll) fillings.

Basil (**daun kemangi**) is available as different varieties. Ordinary sweet basil has the most rounded aroma for *ulam* (vegetable and herb) dishes. Thai holy basil, lemon basil, and purple basil have more specific uses in other cuisines.

Beancurd (**tofu**) is coagulated soymilk, available firm or soft. **Soft beancurd** (*tau huay*) is slippery and tends to crumble easily but has a more silky texture and refined flavor. It is eaten as a breakfast dish or snack. **Firm beancurd** stays in shape when cut or cooked, and has a stronger, slightly sour taste. A variety of this is coarse tofu (*tau kwa*), from which deep-fried crinkly-skinned *tau pok* is made. Thin, sweetened, compressed wafers of beancurd (*teem chok*) are used for Chinese vegetarian dishes. **Beancurd skin** is the thin layer of soy protein that forms on the surface of soybean milk while it is being boiled to make beancurd; this layer is then lifted off and dried. **Fermented beancurd** — white fermented (*foo yee*) and red fermented (*lam yee*) — is used as a condiment or seasoning.

Beansprouts (*tow gay*) are the sprouts of green mung beans, ubiquitous in all Asian cuisines.

Belimbing is a small, powerfully sour starfruit resembling a mini jade-green cucumber. It must be salted before cooking to remove bitter juices.

Buah petai (stink beans) are small, flat jade-green beans about the same size as fava beans, with a slightly sulphurous taste. Usually sold still in their long pods or shelled, in bags.

Bunga kantan (torch ginger) has pale pink spearlike buds; it belongs to the ginger family and has a warm, flowery fragrance. Used shredded in salads and *sambals*.

Bunga telang (butterfly pea) flowers, picked fresh from their vine or dried, yield a vivid indigo blue juice when crushed in water, that is used for coloring various *kueh* (savory cakes).

Candlenuts (*buah keras* or *kemiri*) are oily nuts resembling scuffed macadamias and give curries an unctuous sweetness. They go rancid quickly so buy small packets and refrigerate them. Cashews are the closest substitute.

Cardamom is sold ground, or as small moss-green ridged pods, which contain sticky black seeds with a heady, sweet camphorous scent. An essential Indian and Arabic spice.

Chilies are an indispensable part of Asian cuisine. Most commonly used in Singapore are big chilies, for bulk and flavor, and chili padi (bird's-eye chilies), for gloriously numbing heat. Indian shops typically sell at least 3 or 4 kinds of dried chilies, used variously for heat, color, and pungency.

Chinese cabbage (*tientsin* cabbage, napa cabbage, *bok choy*) has fat, bulbous white ridged stems topped with a froth of crinkly pale green leaves, prized more for its succulence than its rather mild but sweet taste.

Chinese celery looks similar to the flat-leafed parsley, and has a stronger flavor than celery. It is used in soups, stir-fries, and stews.

Chinese chives (*koo chai*) have juicy round stalks tipped with light green buds. Usually stir-fried as a vegetable. Distinct from the flat-bladed Asian chives that are bigger than but taste much like the European kind.

Chinese mushrooms are closely related varieties of shiitake, sold fresh or dried. The best of either are plump and heavy. High-grade dried mushrooms are expensive, but worth it for their luxurious succulence when braised or steamed. If using dried mushrooms, soak in hot water 10 to 15 minutes to soften, then drain. Remove the stems and discard. Cloud ear mushrooms (*muk yee*), also known as wood ear mushrooms, are black curls of dried fungus that expand into dark brown, gelatinously crunchy-textured flaps when soaked.

Cinnamon (*kayu manis*) is less often used in Asia than cassia bark, which is thicker and more pungent than true cinnamon.

Cloves contribute a crucial nuance in five-spice powder and in many Chinese, Indonesian, and Indian dishes.

Cockles (*see hum, kerang*) are also known as blood cockles or blood clams. They are usually very briefly blanched or fried before being eaten.

Coconut has many uses. The water inside makes a cooling drink; the young meat a jelly-like dessert; the mature meat a source of milk for curries or an ingredient itself when grated and fried. Freshly grated is best, but it goes rancid quickly if not used up fast or frozen.

Coriander (*daun ketumbar*, cilantro, or Chinese parsley) has feathery leaves with a clean green aroma and flavor. The roots, beloved by Thai cooks, are intensely sweet-peppery-pungent.

Coriander seeds are small, round, off-white seeds that are best when freshly roasted and crushed, as their warm, nutty, slightly citrus-like aroma is brought out.

Crabs are a favorite food of Singaporeans, and the two most common varieties are large Sri Lankan crabs with dark green-brown shells and meaty claws, and the smaller flower or mottled crabs, with attractive blue and white shells.

Cumin seeds are dusky brown ridged seeds with a penetrat-

ched kangkong (water convolvulus)

Penang *blachan*

tamarind pulp

chili padi (bird's eye chilies)

dried shrimp

gula melaka (Malaccan palm sugar)

candlenuts (*buah keras*)

ikan bilis (baby anchovies)

bangkwang (yam bea[n])

tiger prawns

ladies' fingers (okra)

hae koh (shrimp sauce)

star anise

shallots

white radish (daiko[n])

buah petai (stink beans)

Thai salted radish (*chai poh*)

OTAK UDANG
PRAWN PASTE

ingly pungent, earthy scent. Best toasted and ground fresh.

Curry leaves are fingernail-sized, diamond-shaped leaves that grow in feathery sprigs. They have a warm, balsam-like character.

Dumpling skins made from wheat flour are either square (*won ton*) or round (*sui gow*).

Fennel seeds are small, pale green, ridged seeds with a sweet liquorice aroma.

Fenugreek seeds are tiny ochre-hued seeds with a very strong, warm aroma. Commonly used in fish and seafood curries.

Fish commonly used in the recipes are as follows:
  Batang is distantly related to mackerel, tuna, and swordfish and tastes a little like all of them. It has dark skin and pinky-grey flesh that cooks to a delicious firm white flakiness.
  Pomfret is a diamond-shaped, flat-bodied fish. White pomfret (*bawal puteh*, *cheong yu*) are best steamed, while the smaller, coarser-fleshed black pomfret (*bawal hitam*) are best deep-fried.
  Snapper (*ikan merah*, *angoli*) belongs to a family of related species, of which the big-mouthed, rosy-skinned red snapper is the best known. Its firm but delicate white flesh serves deep-frying, steaming, or grilling equally well.
  Soon hock (marble goby) is a dapple-skinned fish with pearly white flesh that flakes beautifully when steamed or deep-fried.
  Ikan kurau (threadfin, *ma yau yu*, *ngoh her*) is quite possibly the most prized of all fish in our local markets, for its richly flavored, tender flesh. Usually seen in markets

as pinkish-white steaks only, as the fish is very large.
  Snakehead (*sang yue*) is a voracious breeder and feeder with a black-skinned round body and flat, ugly face that quite belies its succulent, fine-flavored flesh, which is wonderful sliced thin and stir-fried, or eaten with noodles in milky soup.
  Stingray (*ikan pari*, *hung her*) is a dense-fleshed fish good for grilling or curries. Only the meaty "wings," ribboned with soft bones, are sold and eaten.
  Tilapia is a red or silvery freshwater fish with soft, mild flesh, but inferior specimens can sometimes taste muddy.

Fishballs and **fishcakes** are made from fish meat pounded with seasoning and salt (and sometimes a filler starch), and made into crunchily resilient balls or oblong cakes, then boiled or deep-fried. Japanese supermarkets typically sell the widest range.

Fish sauce (*nam pla*) is most essential to Thai and Vietnamese cuisine, but is also used across southern China. Pungent in the bottle, it lifts and enhances the savoriness of a dish subtly but thoroughly.

Five-spice powder is a mix of ground star anise, fennel, cloves, cinnamon, and pepper, and is used as a piquant seasoning for stews, braises, and marinades.

Galangal (*lengkuas*, *laos* root, blue ginger) is a hard root with pink-budded tips and ivory skin striped by faint brown lines. It has a uniquely floral, gingery, almost jasmine-like scent.

Ginger is used for pungency and heat when old and thick-skinned. Tender, ivory-colored

young ginger is valued for gentle warmth and its ability to combat richness.

Ginkgo nuts are bittersweet oval yellow-green nuts from the ginkgo tree, much beloved by Japanese and Chinese alike. Often used in Chinese herbal preparations. Nowadays conveniently sold cooked and vacuum-packed.

Black moss fungus (*fatt choi*) is a fine, hair-like dried sea moss, valued in Chinese cooking. Soak in warm water before using.

Hoi sin sauce is a sweet, thick bean sauce, used as a condiment in Peking duck pancakes or as a seasoning in fried noodles and pork stews.

Ikan bilis (baby anchovies) are tiny members of the whitebait family fish, about 5 cm (2 in) long, are usually sold dried. Remove their heads and scrape their bellies clean of any black residue before cooking. They are sometimes sold split and cleaned, in which case just wipe them with damp kitchen paper. The even smaller, ghostly white fish sold fresh in some markets is another whitebait species typically cooked with rice congee or fried into an omelette.

Nangka (jackfruit) is a large tropical fruit, often over a foot across and over 2 feet long, with rough, bumpy skin. Unripe and starchy, it is treated as a vegetable and cooked in curries. Ripe, it turns butter-yellow and pungent-sweet, and is eaten raw.

Kaffir lime leaves (*daun limau purut*) are glossy, dark green, leathery double-lobed leaves that release a strong balsam-lime scent when torn.

Kai lan (Chinese kale) is typically stir-fried with garlic and/or oyster sauce. Both the small baby heads and large mature heads of this crunchy-stalked, perky-leafed vegetable are delicious.

Kangkong (water convolvulus) is a hollow-stemmed water vegetable with long, narrow leaves, widely used across Southeast Asia. Wash well before using to remove grit.

Laksa leaves (*daun kesom*) are spear-shaped leaves that wilt quickly once plucked off the stem, with an intense fragrance reminiscent of lemon with a hint of eucalyptus.

Lard is rendered pork fat. Essential in many Chinese dishes for flavor, and in *dim sum* pastries, also for flaky textures. The brown cracklings left over after rendering lard are called *chee yow char* in Cantonese and are used to garnish many fried and soup noodle dishes.

Lemongrass (*serai*) has pale yellow-green woody shoots that have a powerful lemony fragrance, sharp, and spicy. Absolutely indispensable for most Asian cuisines.

Limes (*limau*) commonly used in Singapore are *limau nipis*, which are golf-ball-sized and also known as key limes, and smaller and more aromatic calamansi limes, with yellow-green skin and orange flesh.

Long beans (snake beans) are unruly two-feet long beans with rough-textured pale green skin and delicious flavor.

Longans are juicy white fruit the size of large cherries with black stones and mustard-brown shells. Very commonly sold in cans. Chinese dry goods stores sell whole dried unshelled longans, and also shelled, stoned raisin-sized nuggets of longan meat.

Lotus seeds (*lien chi*) are fat yellow seeds taken from the large pods left by fallen lotus flowers. A symbol of fertility used in both sweet and savory dishes. Nowadays sold canned or cooked and vacuum-packed.

Mung bean vermicelli (glass noodles or *tang hoon*) are sold in small or large bundles of translucent threads that become slithery, resilient and transparent when soaked.

Oyster sauce (*ho yow*) are the rich, thick brown extract of dried oysters. Luxe versions made with abalone and vegetarian versions made from mushrooms also exist.

Palm sugar (*gula melaka*) reduced and crystallized sugar palm sap, whose color and intensity vary between regions and seasons. Malay palm sugar comes in hard mahogany brown cakes; Thai palm sugar is softer.

Pandan leaf (screwpine or *daun pandan*) looks like giant grass and indeed smells of new-mown grass and vanilla. Used across Asia to perfume desserts and rice dishes.

Persimmons (*ang kee*) should be eaten only when fully ripe; otherwise they have a sour and astringent taste. The most favored type in Singapore is the bulbous orange kind that ripens to jellylike succulence. Dried, they become flat discs covered with a white bloom, and are used in desserts.

Preserved salted vegetable (*tang chai*) salty, mildly pungent flakes sold in packets or jars. Used to garnish and flavour rice congee and soups.

Preserved salted radish (*chai poh*) is yellow-brown radish and sold chopped or in chunks, used in omelettes, stir-fries, and snack foods.

Preserved sour plums are whole beige plums sold in jars of pickling liquid, used for making drinks or flavoring soups and steamed items.

Rice is a staple food and the most commonly used variety in Singapore is Thai jasmine rice, a delicate, perfumed long grain. Medium-grain white rice is used to make congee, and also cooked in molds to make *ketupat*, compressed rice, to be eaten with satay or Malay curries. The Indian community favors basmati rice.

Rice noodles are always white, but their shapes vary widely, from thin and round (laksa noodles) to short, round and fat (*bee tai mak*), flat and wide (*hor fun, chee cheong fun*) to flat, thin and square (*kway chup*), fine vermicelli-like hanks (*bee hoon*) to tagli-atelle-like ribbons (*kway teow*, which comes in several widths). *Bee hoon* and *kway chup* are sold only dried; *kway teow* both dried and fresh; and the others only fresh.

Salted soybeans of two main kinds are used in Chinese cooking. Wet salt-fermented yellow soybeans (*tau cheo*), which are sometimes sweetened with red dates, season many southern Chinese and Nonya dishes. Dry salted black soybeans (*tau see*) lend a pungent accent to meat and fish dishes.

Sesame oil is extracted from the roasted (darker oil) or raw (lighter oil) seeds. It is used as a seasoning, never as a base oil for stir-fries, as high heat turns it bitter.

Shallots in Asia are small bulbs with maroon skin, with a sweeter, lighter flavor than an onion.

Shaoxing rice wine is a Chinese yellow rice wine made from glutinous rice fermented with yeast. Essential for sauces and marinades. Higher grades can be drunk with food.

Shrimp paste is made from salted, fermented tiny prawns. There are many different varieties, ranging from the creamy purple paste the Cantonese use to marinate chicken and the Vietnamese put on their noodles, to pulpy pink Malaccan *chinchalok* (salted whole krill), dark pink Malaccan blachan, and dark brown, pungent Penang blachan. The latter is an essential ingredient in sambals and spice pastes, has the widest use. *Hae koh* is a tar-like sauce of fermented shrimp, salt, sugar, and thickeners used as a dip or sauce ingredient. All shrimp condiments must be kept in the fridge, in a tightly sealed, completely airtight container.

Soy sauce is brewed from soybeans and sometimes wheat, fermented with salt. Light soy sauce is the saltiest, used as a table dip and cooking seasoning. Dark soy sauce contributes color as well as flavor. Thick dark soy sauce, drizzled on boiled eggs by Chinese everywhere, is made syrupy by caramel or molasses and wheat flour. Thick dark sweet soy sauce,

or *ketjap manis*, is sweetened still further.

Star anise is an eight-pointed star commonly used in Chinese cooking. It is usually added whole and should not be eaten.

Tamarind (*assam*) is characterized by thick stubby brown pods enclosing sweet-sour flesh. It is most commonly sold as packets of moist seed-studded pulp, though some Indian shops sell made-up strained tamarind paste or liquid, and occasionally powder.

Turmeric (*kunyit*) grows in stubby fingers that flash brilliant yellow-orange under dirty-brown skin. It has anti-septic and astringent qualities, and it stains everything permanently, so scrub your knife blade, hands, and chopping board immediately after handling it. Foot-long, spear shaped turmeric leaves (*daun kunyit*) have a fresh, peppery, lemon-balm like scent and are used in *ulam* (vegetable and herb) and seafood dishes.

Wheat noodles may or may not contain eggs; the thinnest, angel-hair type (*mee kia*) and the flat, ribbon-like type (*mee pok*) can be bought fresh or dried, but the yellow noodles used for dry or soup-based Hokkien mee, as thick as a slim chopstick, are only sold fresh.

White fungus (*suet yee*) is sold in off-white heads that look like sponges, which expand into frilly white clouds when soaked in water. Used in savory and sweet Chinese soups for its appealingly resilient texture.

lemon grass

turmeric ↑

angled gourd

belimbing

terigu (white wheat kernels)

dried persimmon ↑

brinjal (Japanese eggplant)   nangka (jackfruit)

peanut brittle

Index of Recipes